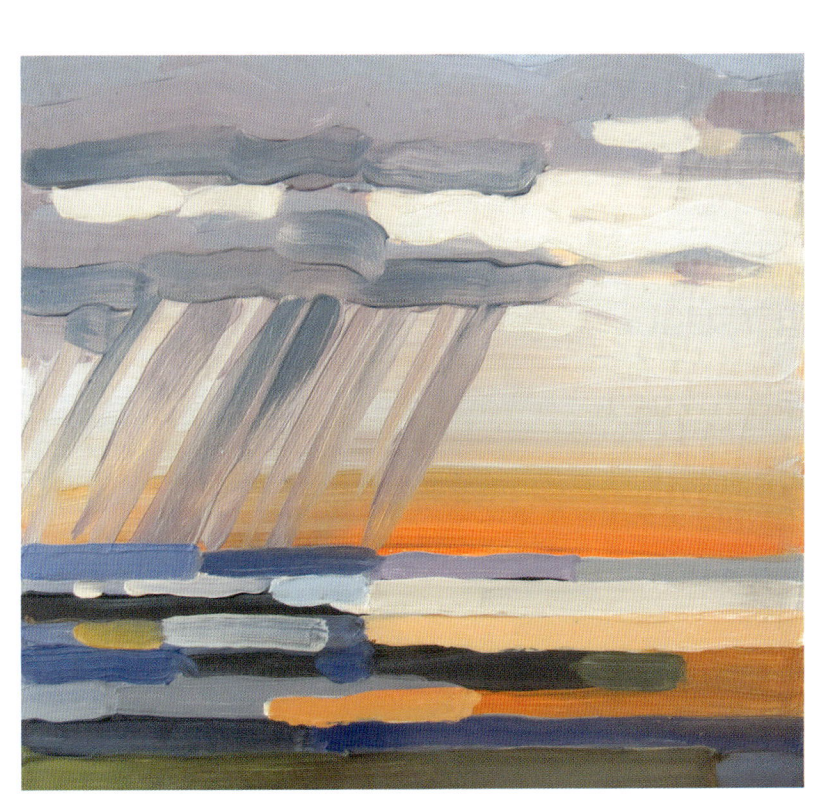

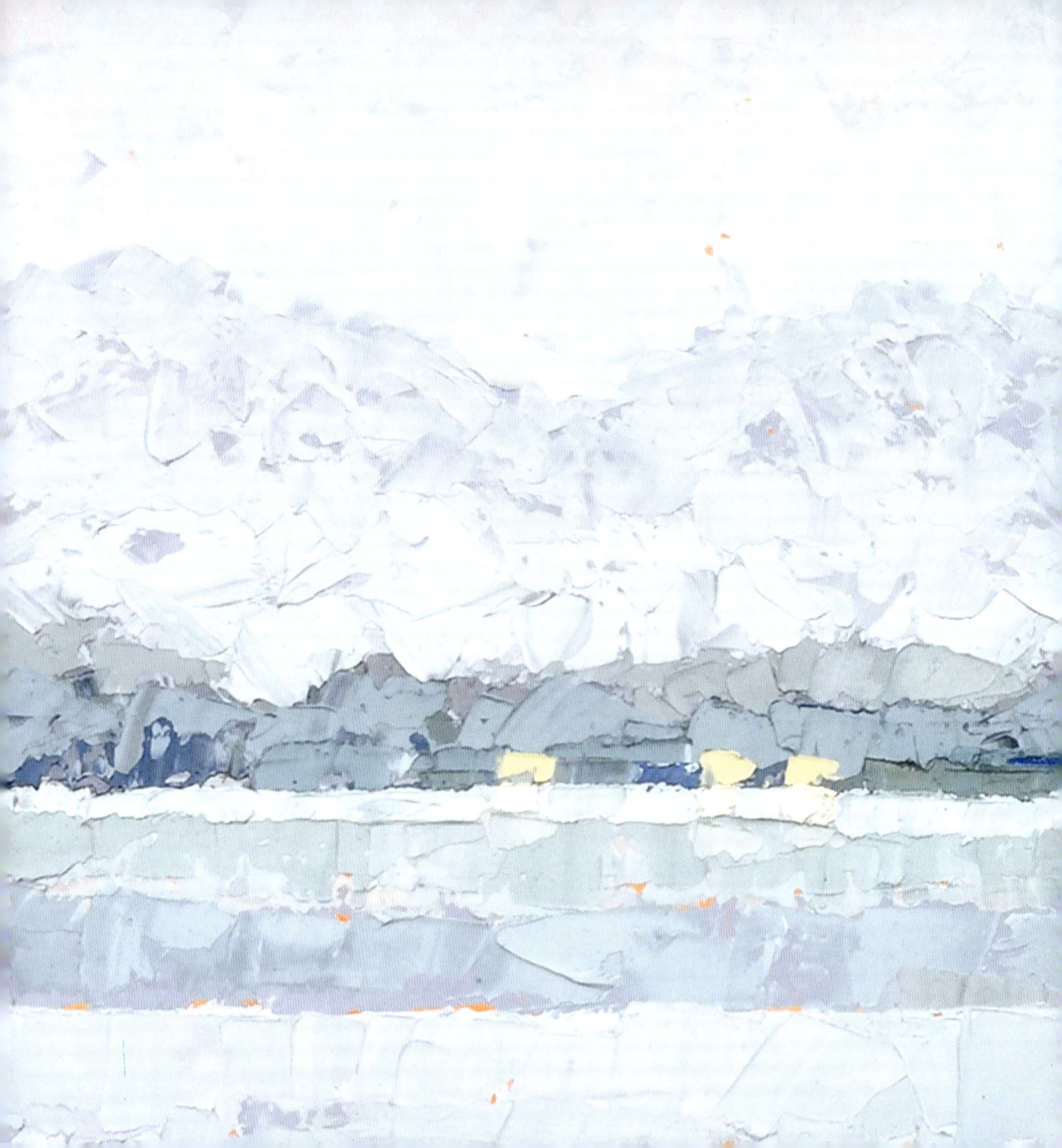

Away to See

Martha's Vineyard

PAUL NORWOOD & LIZ NORWOOD

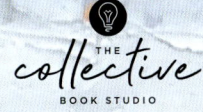

THE
collective
BOOK STUDIO

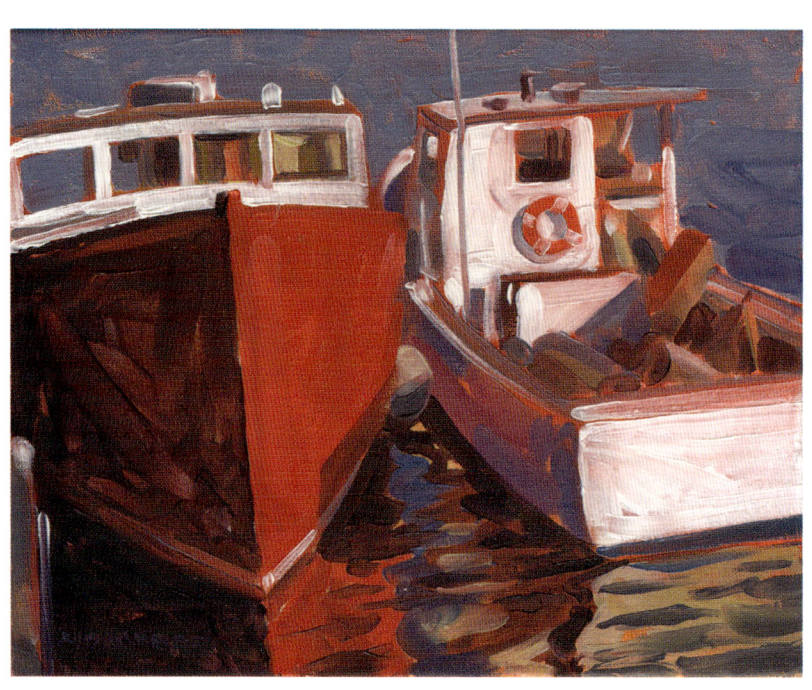

For Jameson and Laina

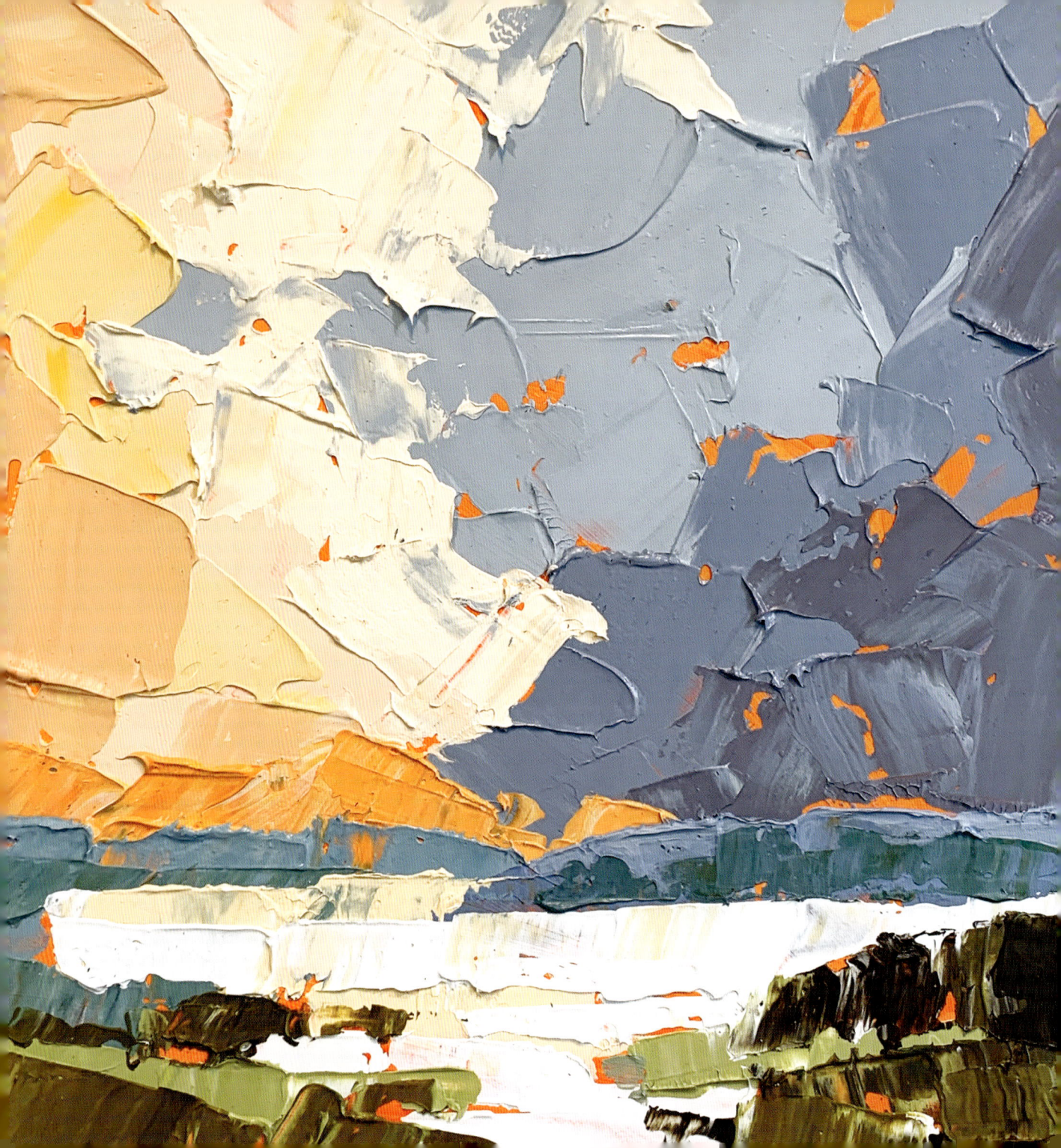

Come Away

We are summer folks, a category of Vineyarder that exists somewhere between the washashores and the day-trippers. We've been lucky enough to return to the Island for thirty-plus years, and in that time we've come to understand some of the truths of this place. The deep thread of history and tradition. The astonishing natural beauty. The notion that sometimes the simplest things bring the greatest joy.

We've also come to discover our favorite corners and experiences, some of which we share with you in this book. For us, the act of painting and writing our travels ushers us into another mindset, where we can turn off the autopilot, be curious, pay attention. Because sometimes the best way to see what's right in front of us is to get away from the everyday. *Away to See* is a creative exploration of that "away" state of mind.

If you've never been to Martha's Vineyard, we invite you into these pages to dip your toes in new waters. If you've had the great fortune to spend days, weeks, months or even years here, we hope they nudge you to see the familiar in a new way. This book is a handful of Island moments, in no particular order. Which is how we hope you'll enjoy it.

Liz & Paul

An Invitation

There are many facets
to the Vineyard.

Each one bends and blends
climates and cultures
terrain and topography
artists and authors
farmers and fishers
tribe and tribulation
land and sea
history and legend.

Each facet a proposal
to roam
to explore
to dive in.

Each facet a mere drop
in the ocean of this place.

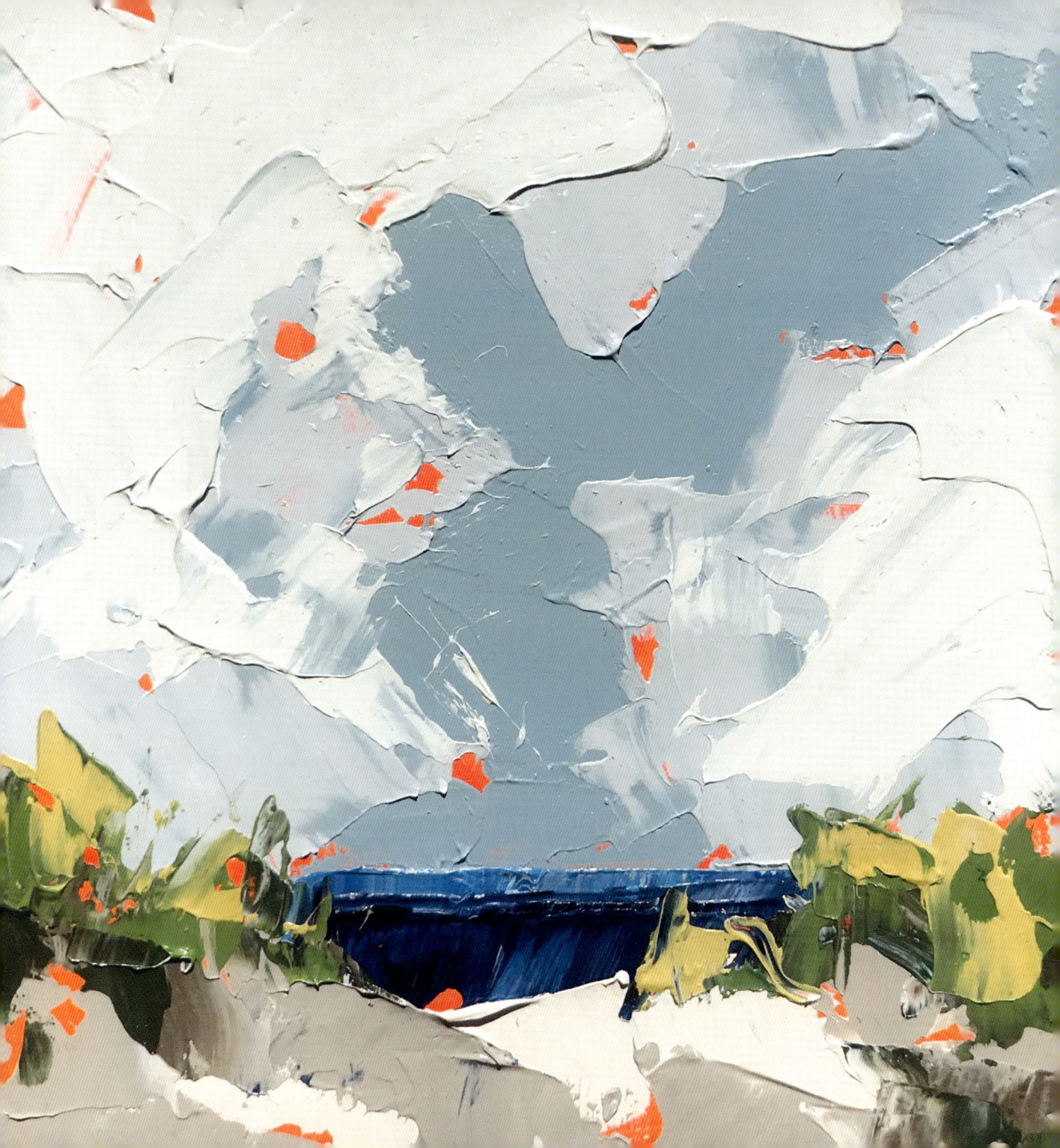

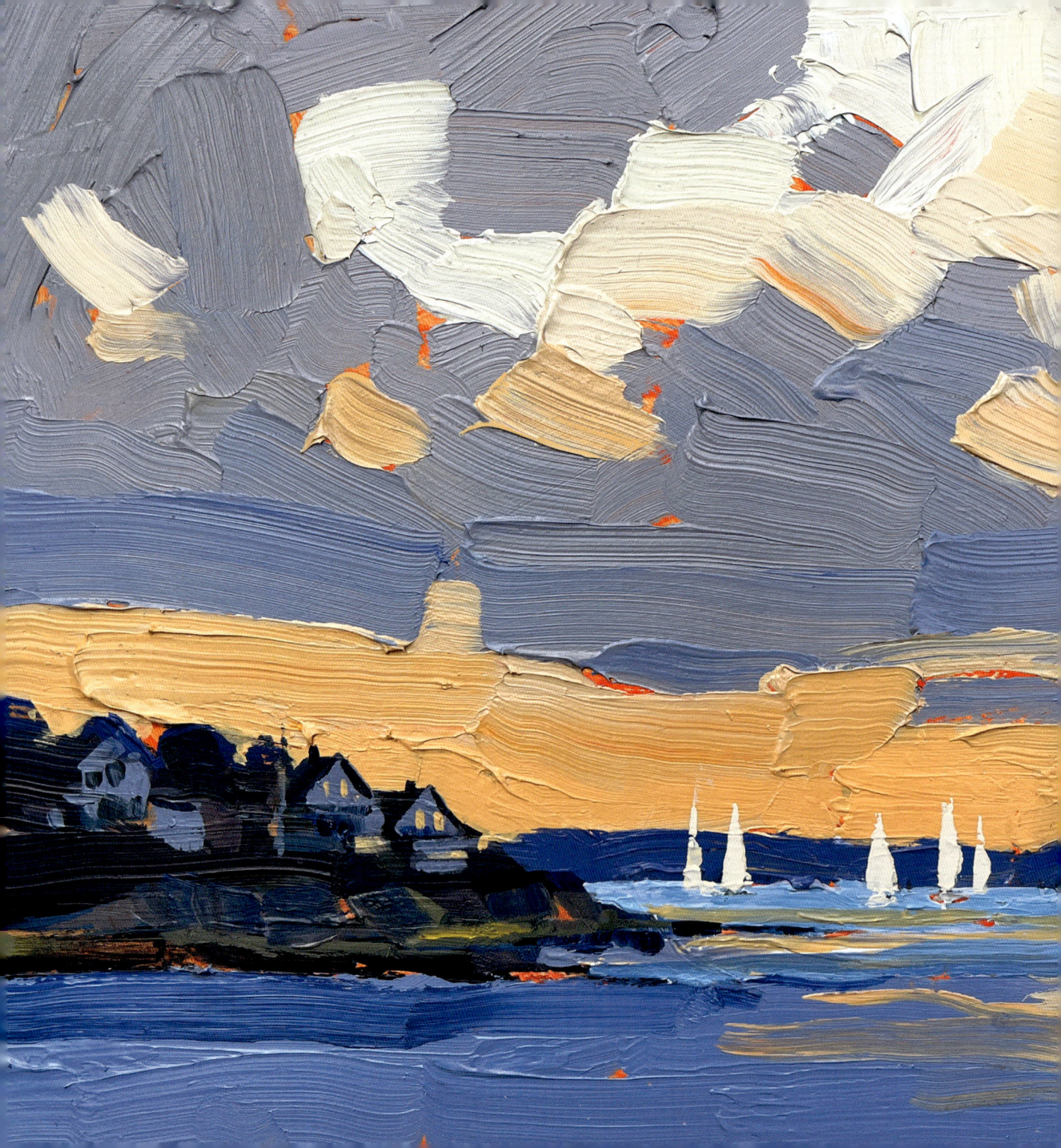

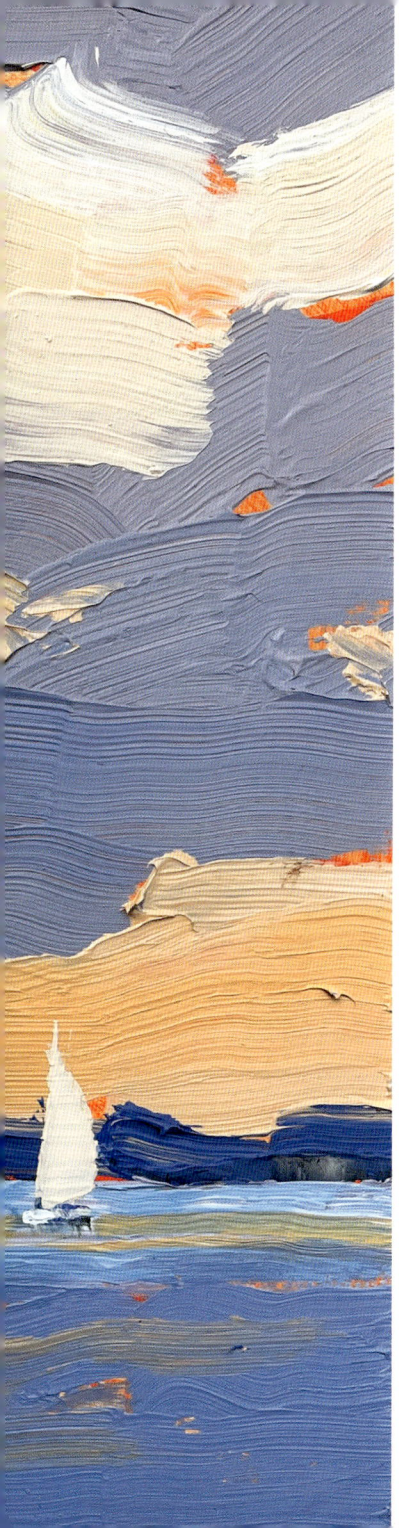

Are We There Yet?

riding waves of Sound
liquid portal ship to shore
we are delivered

Simple Life

Every spring, slight adjustments.

To showering outdoors, when outdoors is 48 degrees
and there is no indoor shower.

To the hotplate that blows the fuse if both burners
are on at the same time as the toaster.

To taking needle and thread
to old sweatshirts and socks
still in fine shape for a beach read
                    a bike ride
                         a trip to the farmstand.
Our small corner of the Island
with small rooms, small drawers, spotty wifi
yet a short walk to a glorious pond
                  a forest of oaks
                     a friend's house.
Being here reminds us
that we are not custodians of our worries
                  our belongings
                    or our calendars.

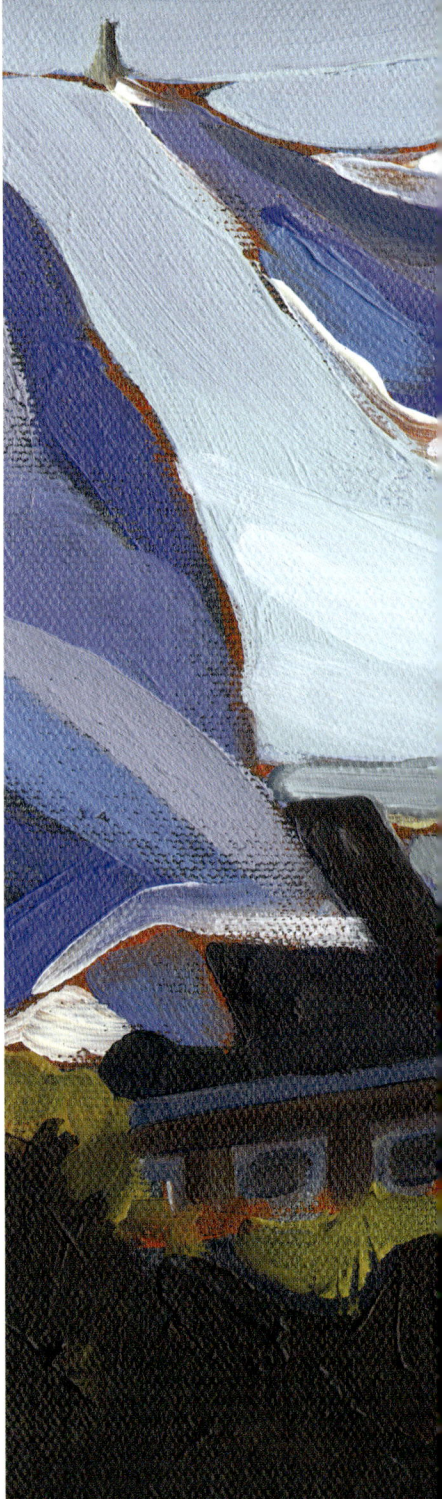

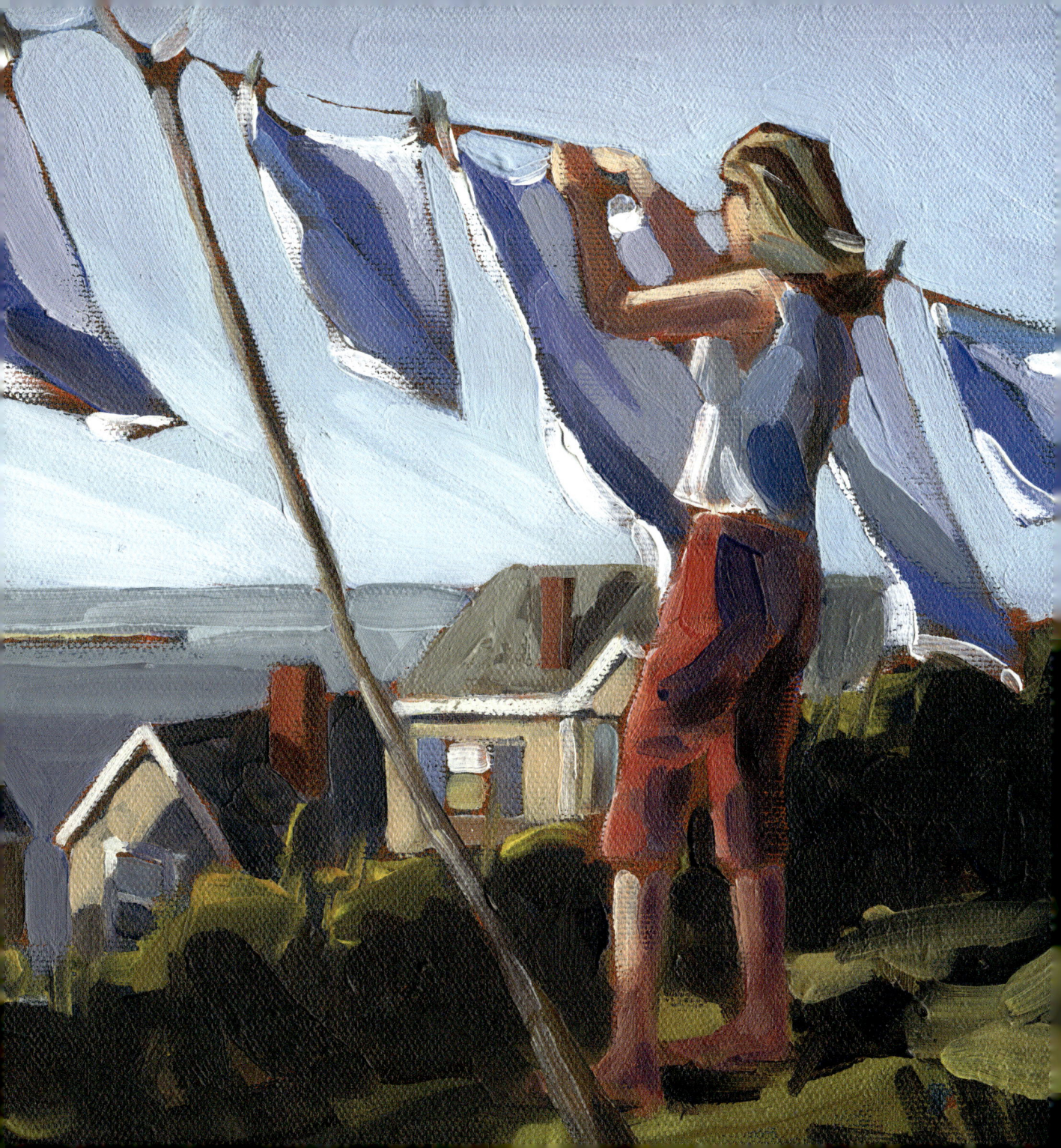

Ode to Prepositions

Cities and towns are lived *in*.
Islands, however, are lived *on*.

So when you're here,
you're *on* Martha's Vineyard.

And when your toes
are planted firmly in the sand,
you can simply say you're
on island.

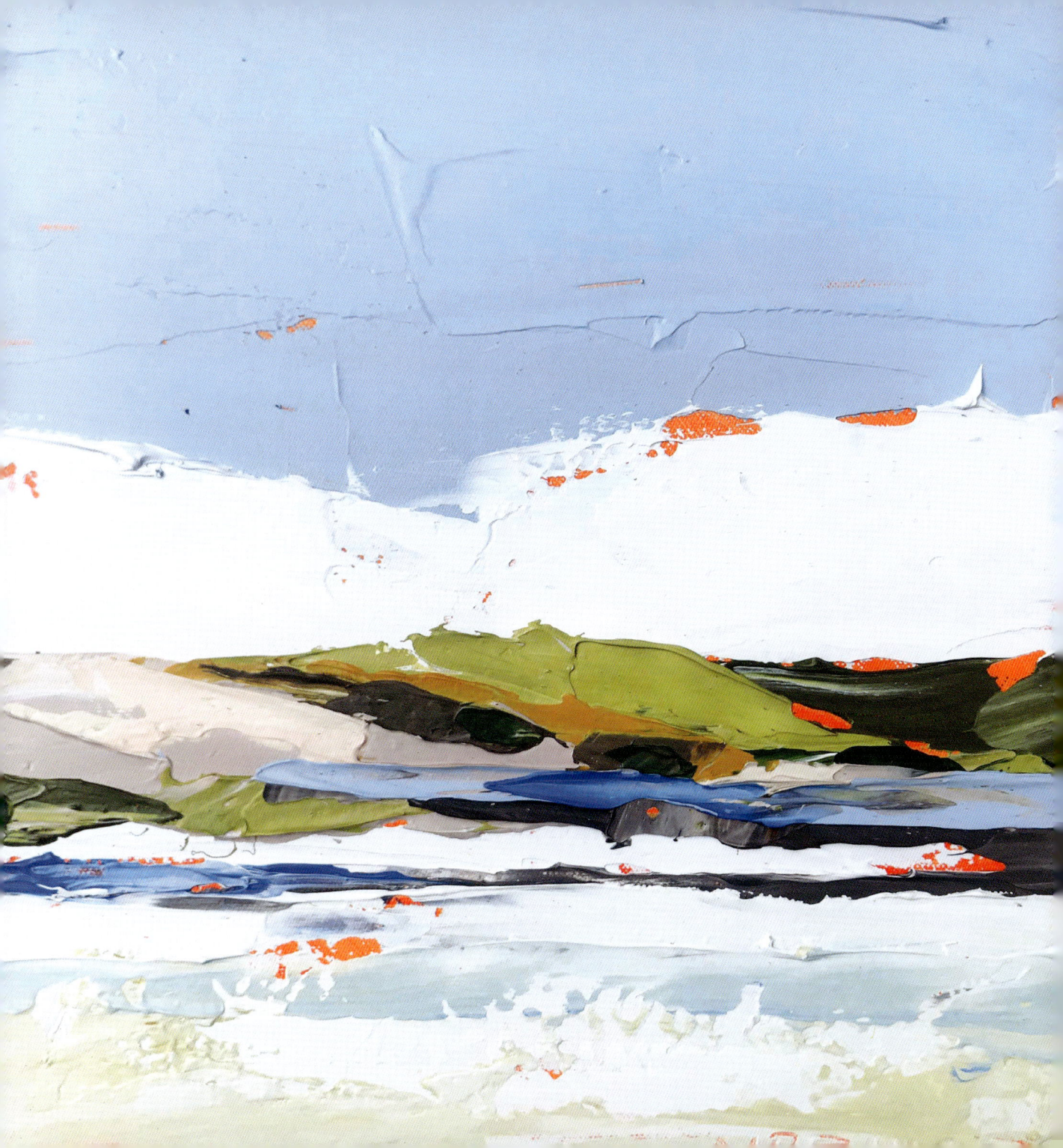

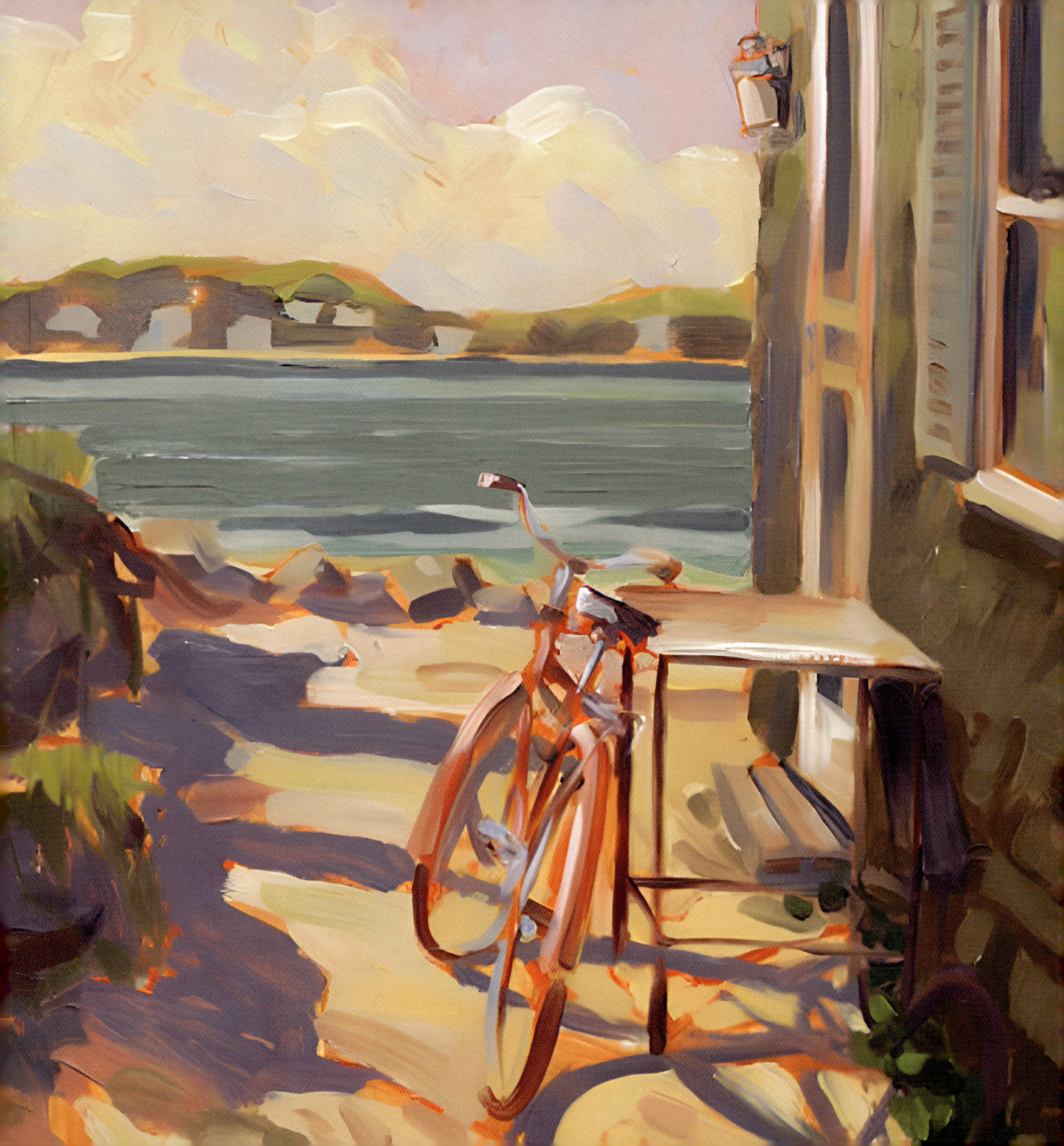

Dropping In

The Island has a distinct *drop-in-anytime* vibe.
Maybe because we can leave our doors unlocked
or maybe we prefer drop-ins to phone calls
because seeing a face attached to a voice
is a beautiful thing in itself.
Maybe it refers to that point in our stay
when we finally start to
drop in
relax
slow down
turn off our phones
and listen for the slap of the screen door
announcing that someone
has decided to drop in.

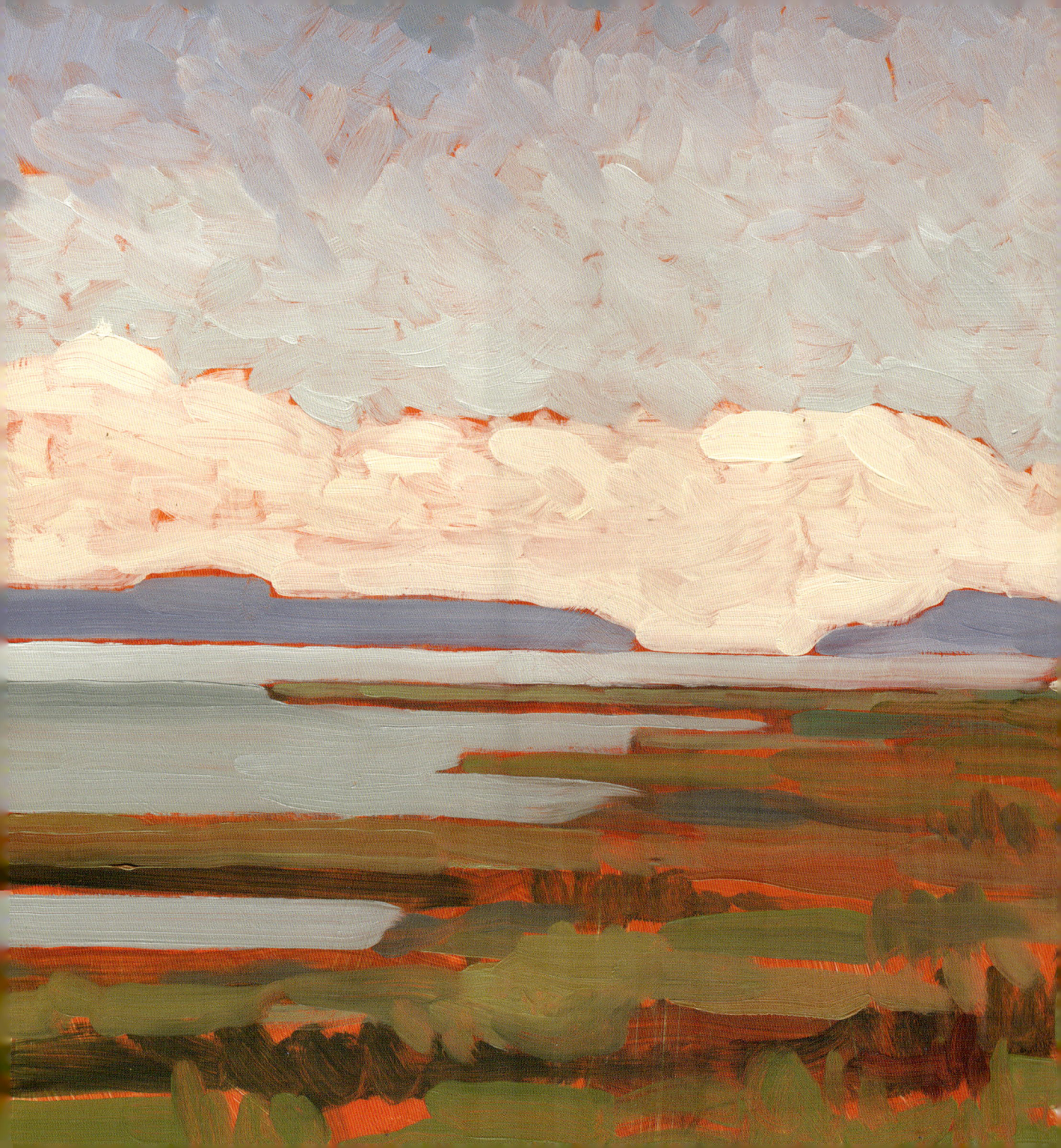

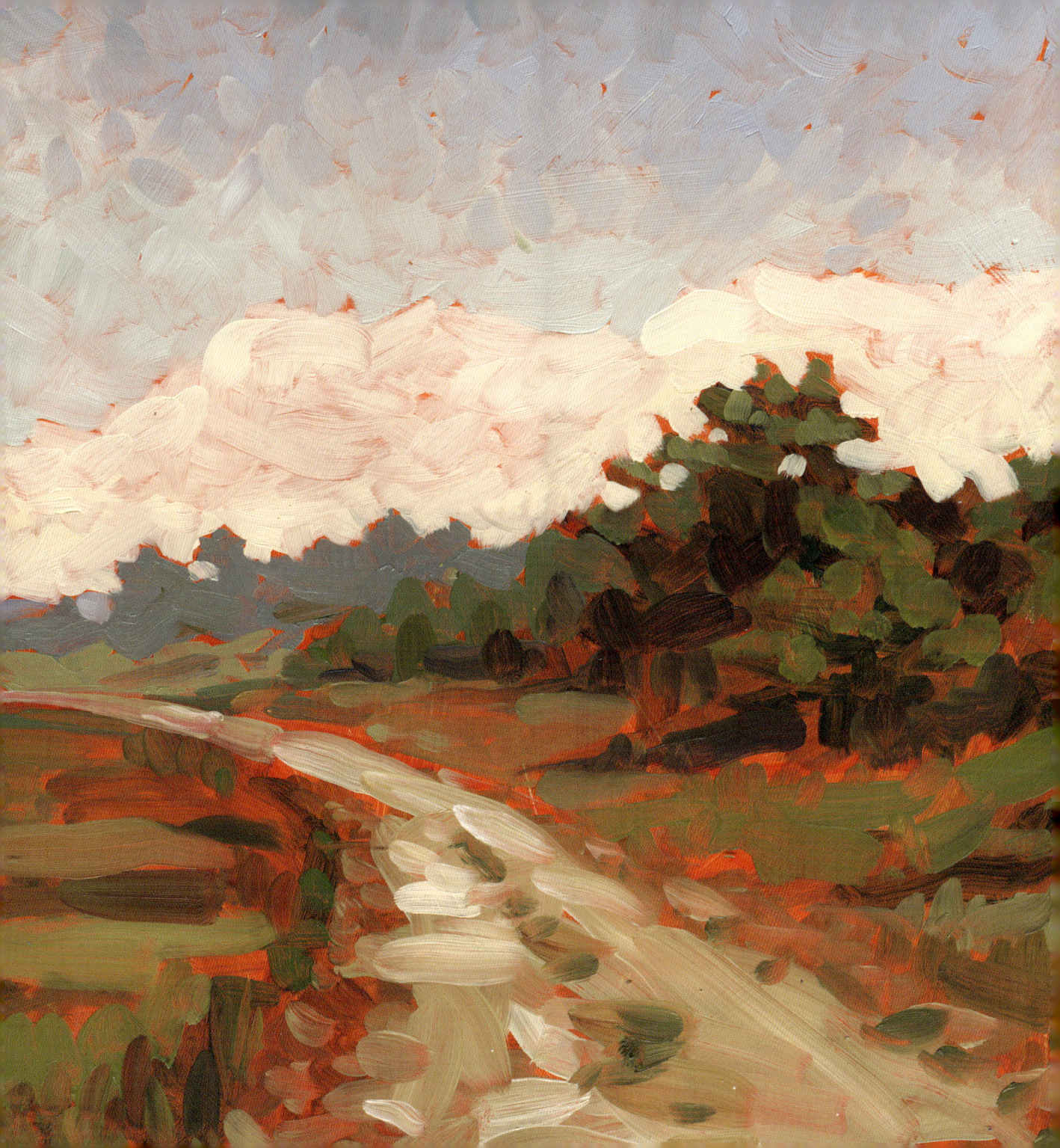

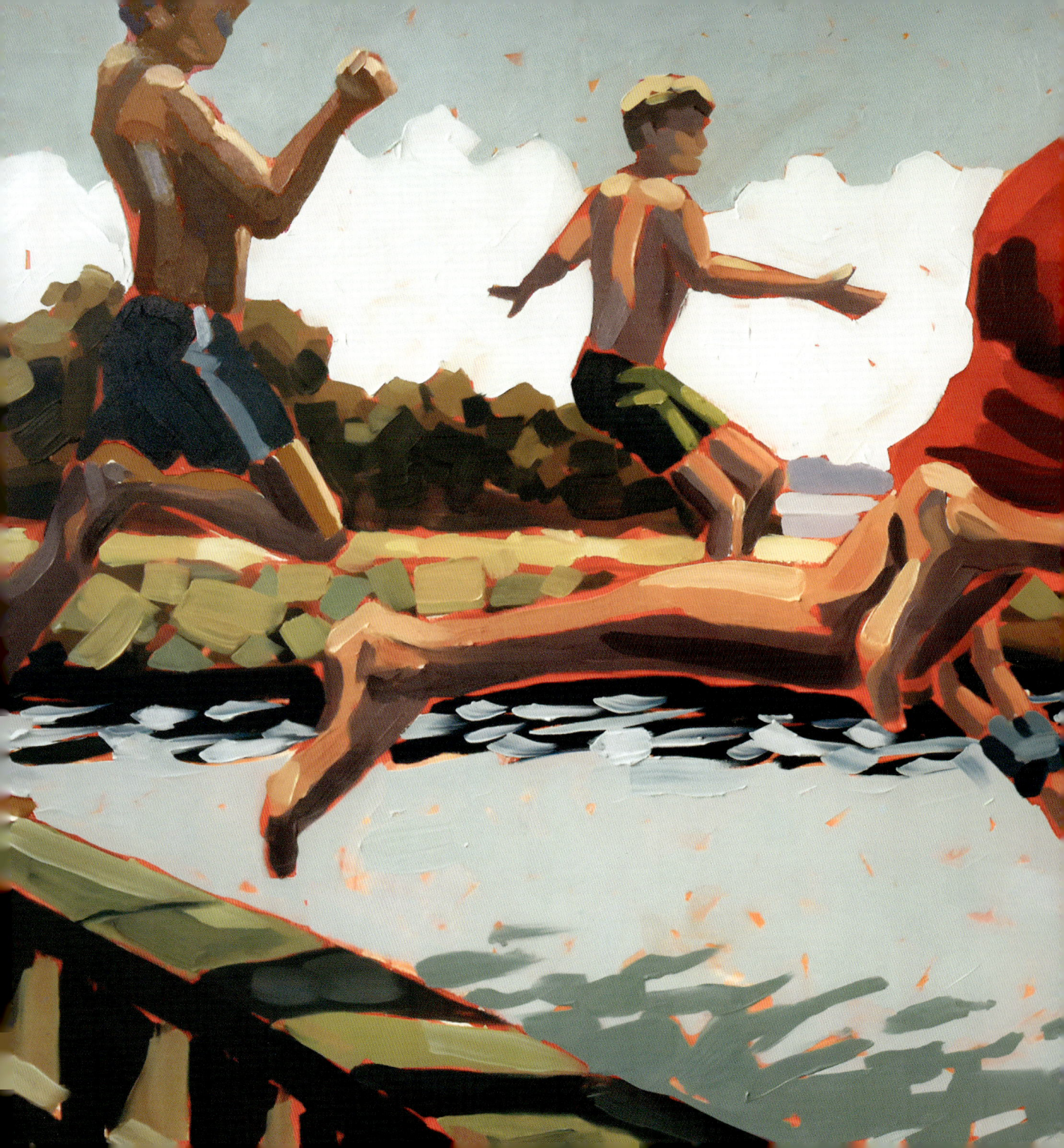

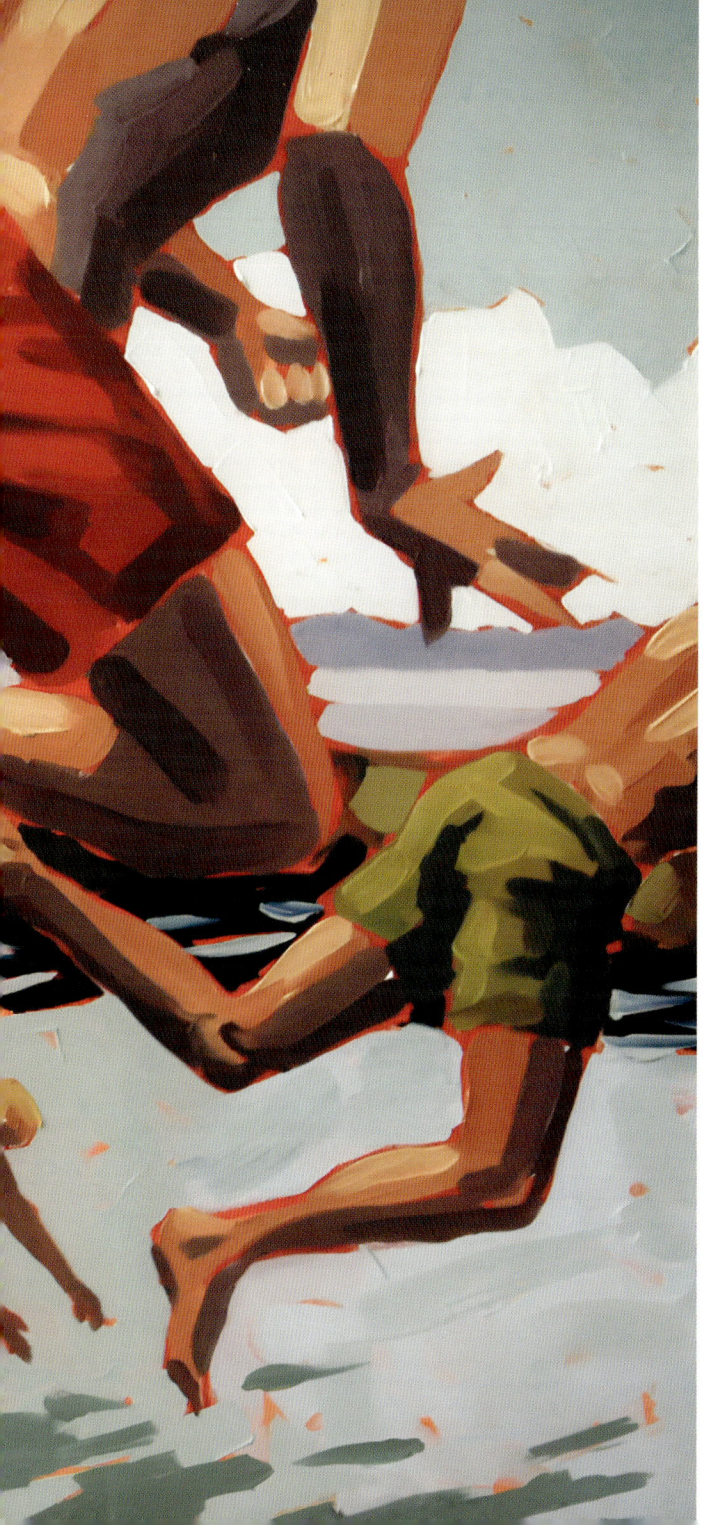

Jaws Bridge

As if the

no-joke

15-foot jump

to the smack of water

and the flinty

seafloor below

wasn't scary enough

they had to

go and name

the bridge after

a man-eating

shark.

Great Pond

The Pond carries the sky on its shoulders, sand tickling its hem,
fingers splayed like the talons of an osprey, knuckles tucked into
secret coves and pocket bays. The air is musty-sweet
with oyster shells and dune grass.

When the sun is high and warm, it's an oasis for swimming, sailing,
fishing. But when darkness arrives, this pond becomes a container
of light in all its infinite iterations.

On any given night the glassy waters reflect
a riot of sunset, moonlight, shooting star, lightning shock,
bioluminescent jellies and dancing fireflies.

We settle in and watch, warming our toes in the shallows
while the planktons and cosmos carry on their hums
into the great forever.

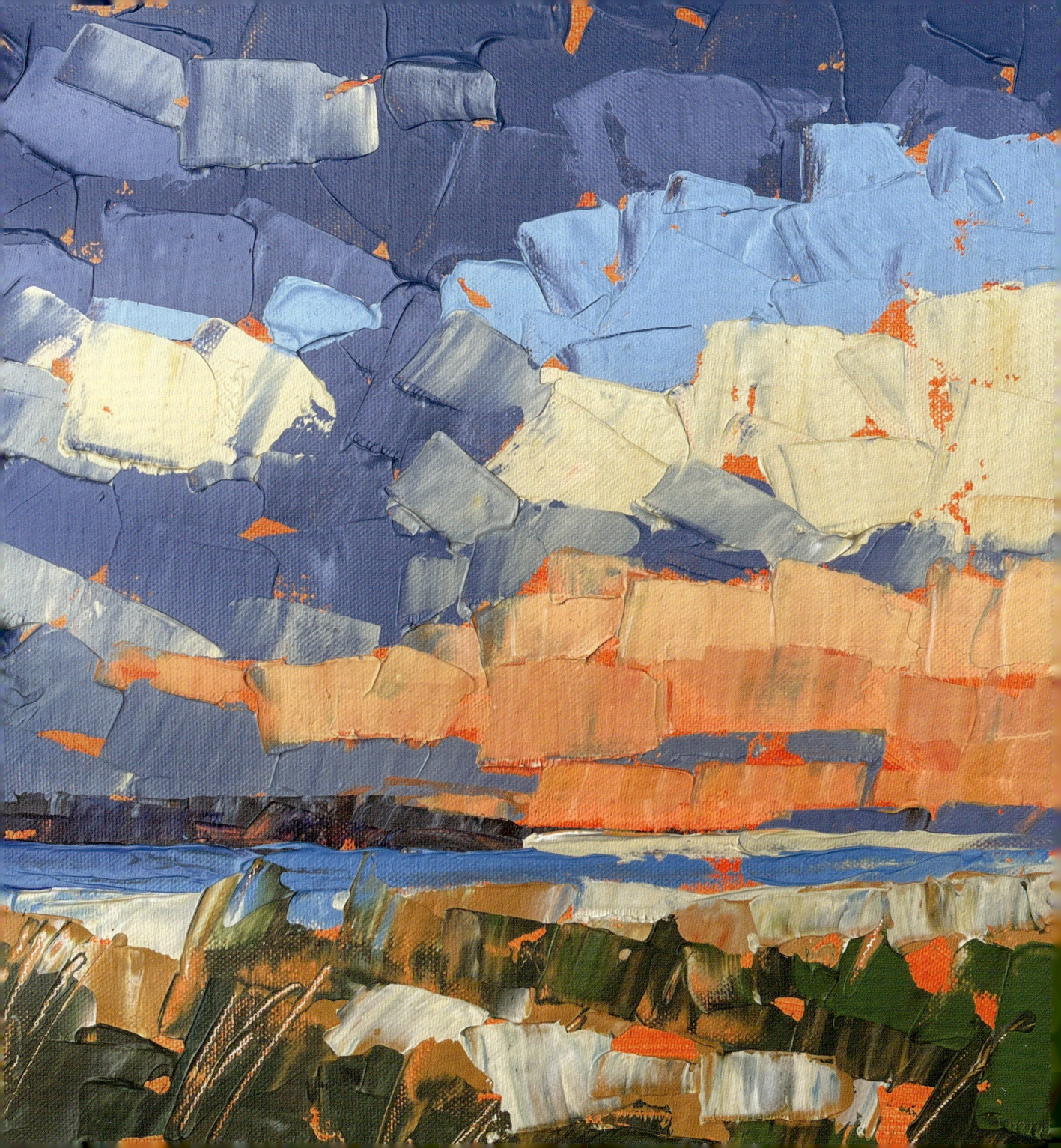

General Store

Back in the day
every town had one.
Part meeting house, part post office
corner pub, church pew, sewing circle.

Staples and sundries
necessities and nice-to-haves
bits and bobs
a kind of self-portrait of a town.

At a time when the notion of
a general store sounds quaint
many here still flourish.

Like little lighthouses
helping us navigate
the everyday.

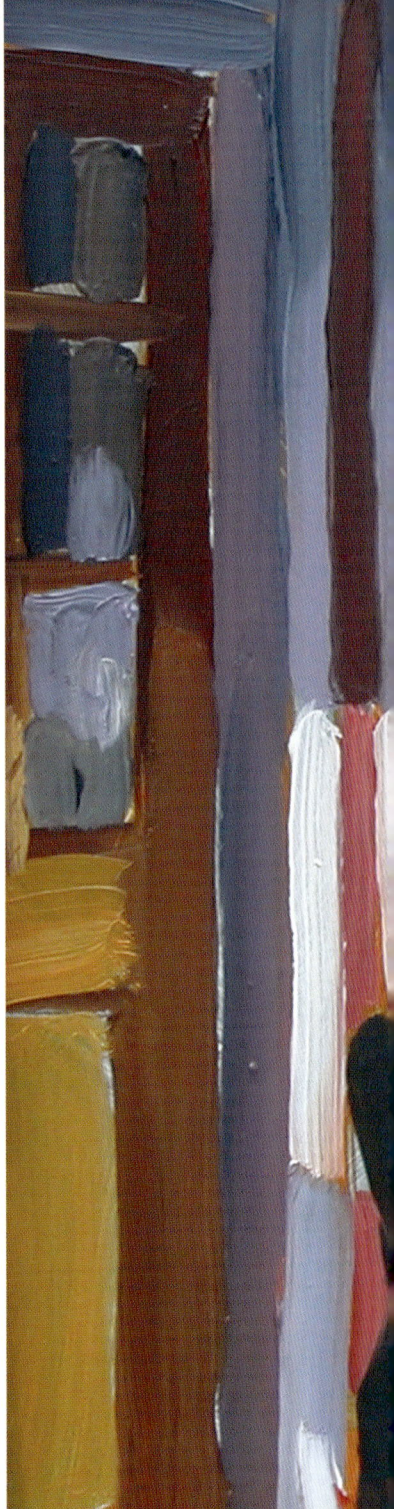

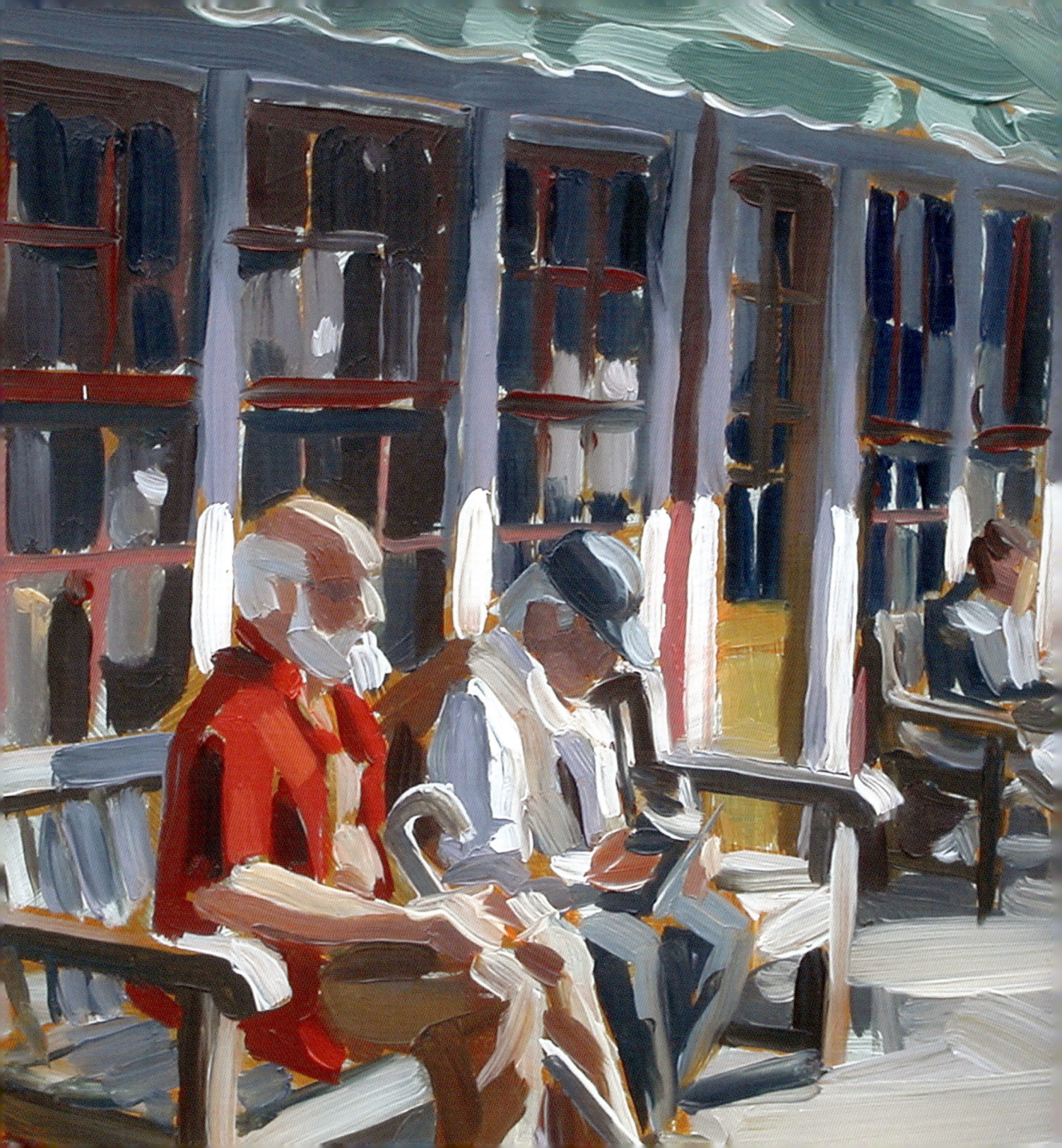

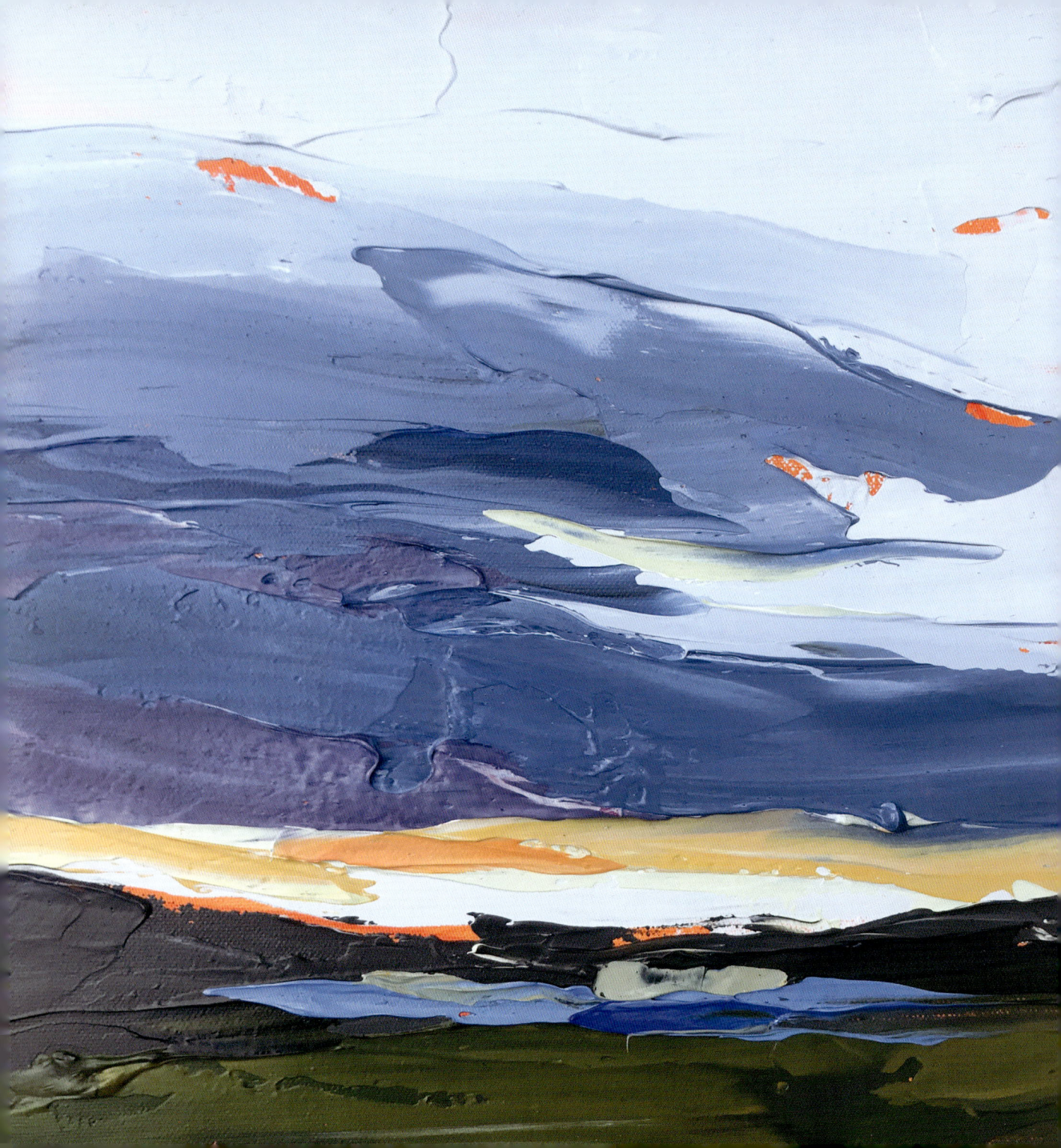

Ice House Pond

She plays hard to get.
Her dirt path is long and prickly
nestled in a fertile and fetching wood.

Getting here feels a lot like coming to the Island:
rarely easy, sometimes painful, always worth it.

We shed our clothes, jump in feet first
float on our backs, swim in her silence.

The Wampanoag called her *manaquayak*
"safe and secure place."

Something about her
invites contemplation
like a library
or a cathedral
or a secret
that doesn't like
being shared.

The Picnic

Takeout with an ear of corn and a scoop of slaw in a pleated paper cup
is a perfectly respectable way to go. But sometimes we hit the beach
with nothing more than a pair of lobsters, a handful of potatoes,
and a sturdy pot. Maybe a bottle of cheap white.

We forage for driftwood, build the fire. Fill the pot with seawater,
take turns tugging on the wine while we wait for it to boil. Plop, hisssss…
into the pot and the shells quickly crimson. Thread some dune grass
through the pot handles and drain slowly so dinner doesn't land in the sand.

It's never easy. Breaching the prickly exterior 'til our fingers bleed.
Navigating the minefield of innards, bright orange (roe) and green (yep, liver.)
Extracting one by one briny bite: a knuckle here, a flipper there.
Much like shelling pistachios, the effort boosts the payoff.

By the end, we've got seaweed in our teeth, swampy hands, and errant
lobster bits in our hair. Every shred of edible meat is gone. Bellies full.
Who needs a bib and a wet nap when the ocean awaits?

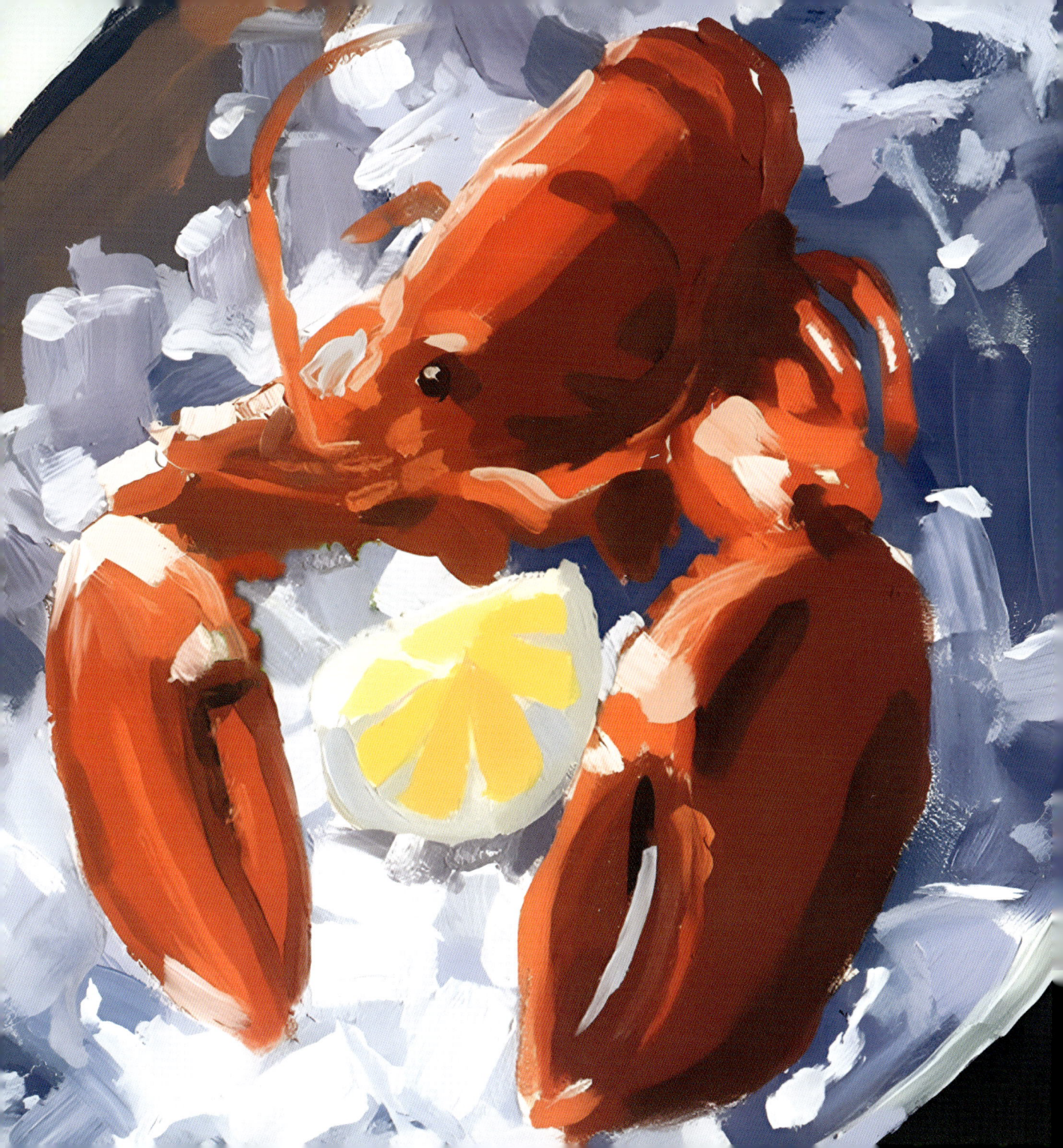

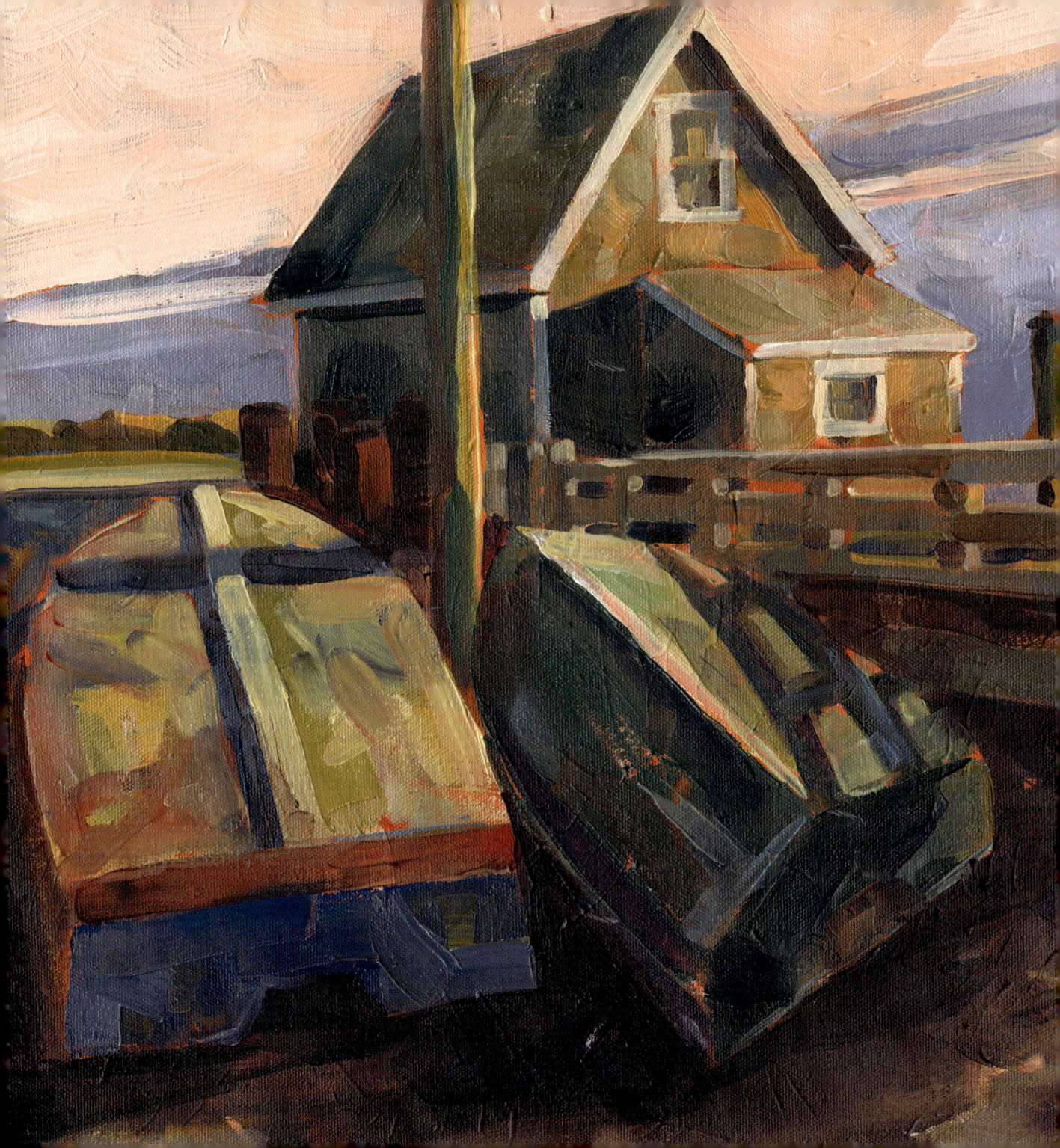

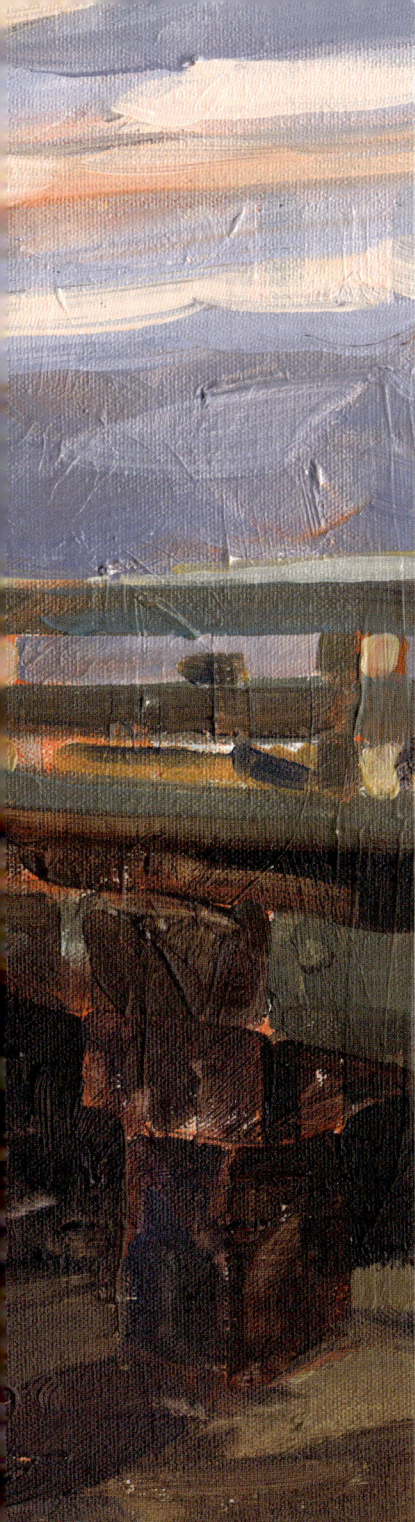

Menemsha

Fishing village. The words themselves are quaint, rustic
conjuring a bygone era of sea shanties, weathered faces
and tendrils of pipe smoke on cold, early mornings.
They harbor stories of storms and struggle, written in
faded buoys, frayed netting, seaweed-crusted traps.
In callused hands and rusty anchors.
In venerable salt-scarred vessels and their captains
who've seen a thing or two at sea.

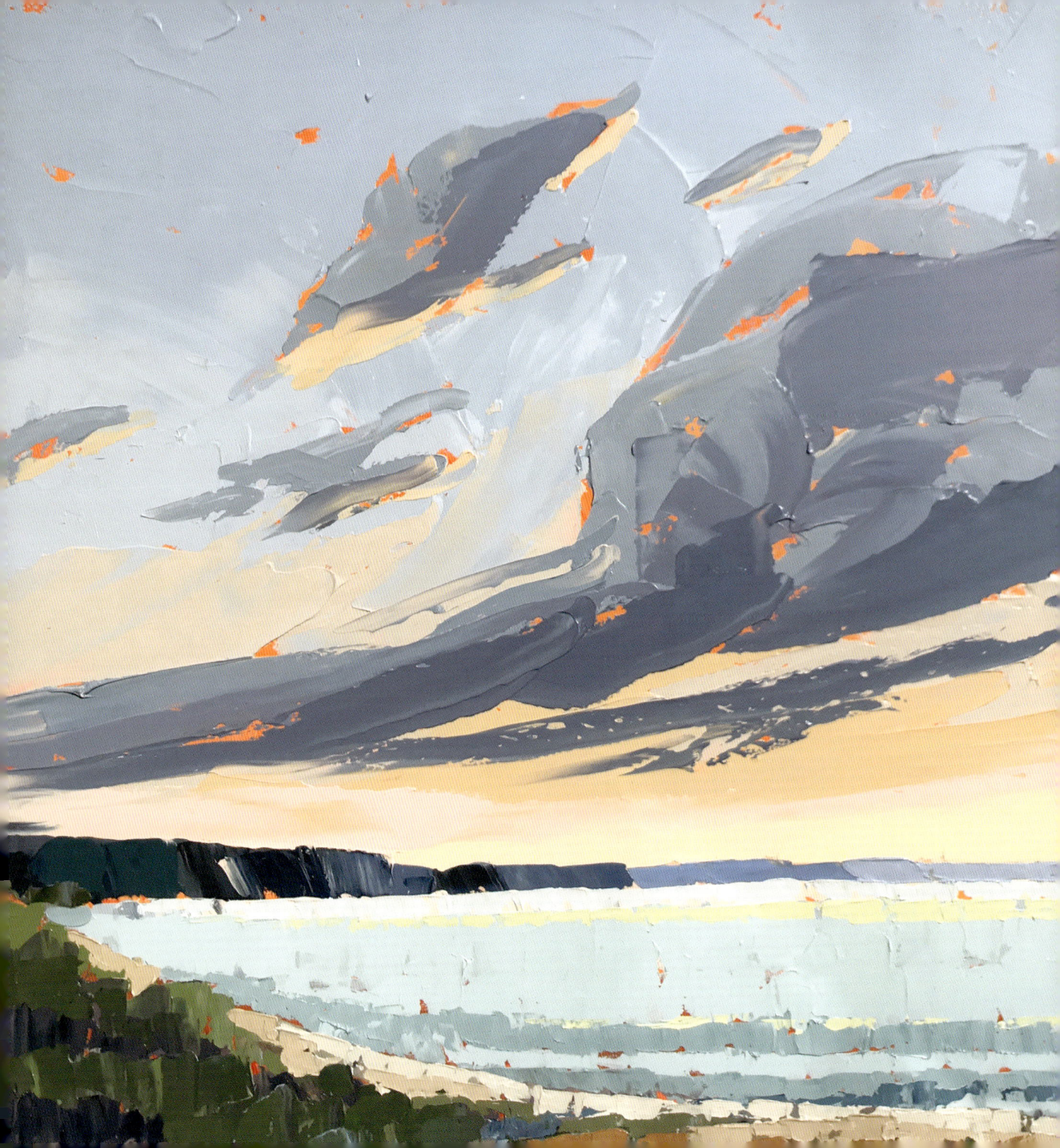

Lambert's Cove

With mackerel clouds setting up to the west
the sunset is on everyone's mind.

A few miles to the east of Menemsha
is a private crescent jewel of sand
only open to interlopers like us after 5pm.

Down the oaken sun-dappled path
just beyond the sandals and flip-flops parked at the door,
a smattering of day people still lazing on the shoreline
settle in for the exact same sunset
viewed by the flocks just a crow's fly away.

The water knows this is a good spot too,
because it's always a little bit warmer here.

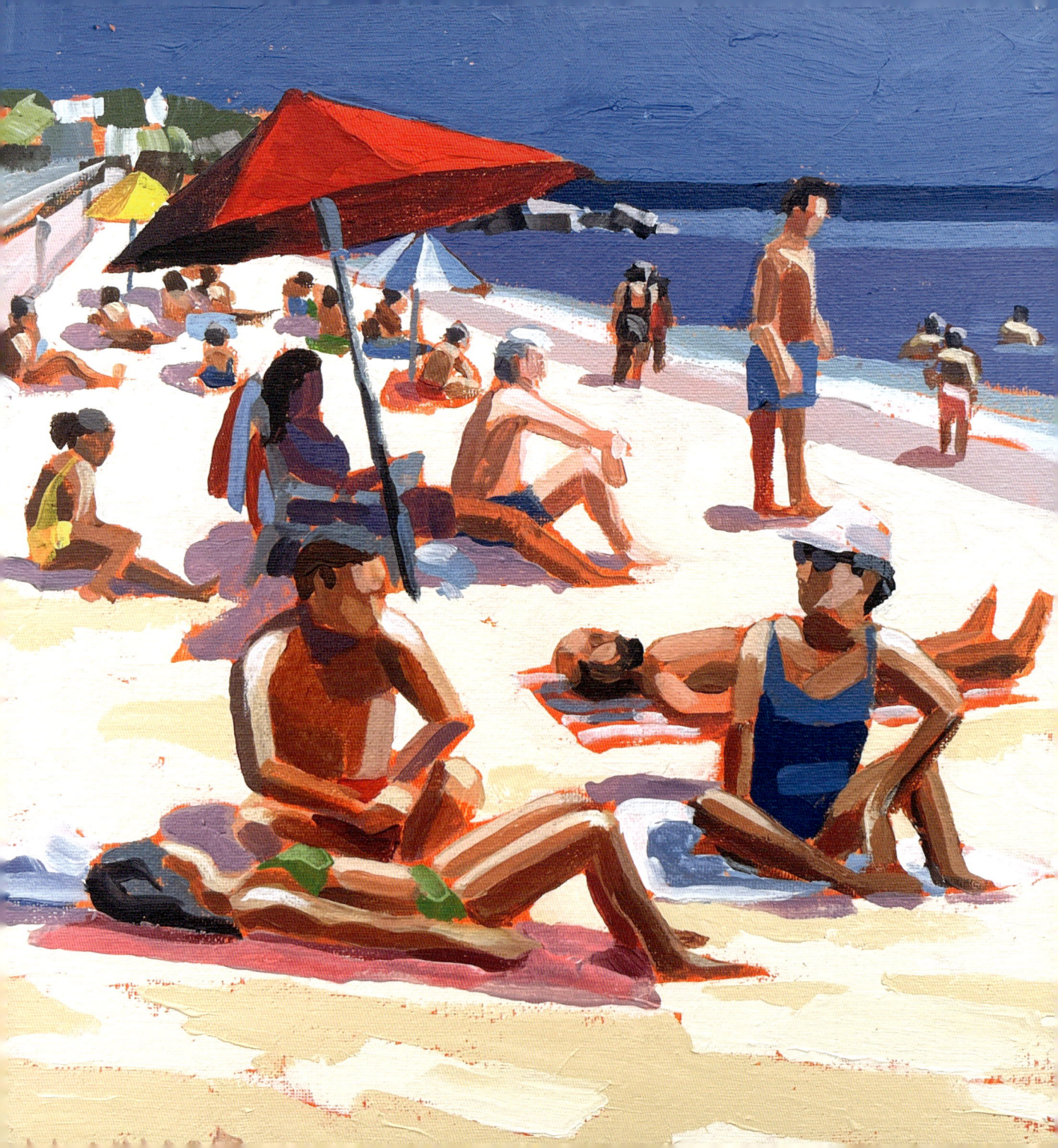

The Inkwell

Its small jetties are fingers
that hold this beach
with a gentle grasp
holding fast the sand
to the vast green of Ocean Park
the maze of gingerbread cottages
and the kinetic energy of Oak Bluffs,
a town that rolled out
the welcome mat for Black people
at a time when many others did not.
What started as a retreat
continues to be
a sacred gathering place,
families and friends
poets and Polar Bears
returning year after year
for generations
to relax
to rejoice
to be.

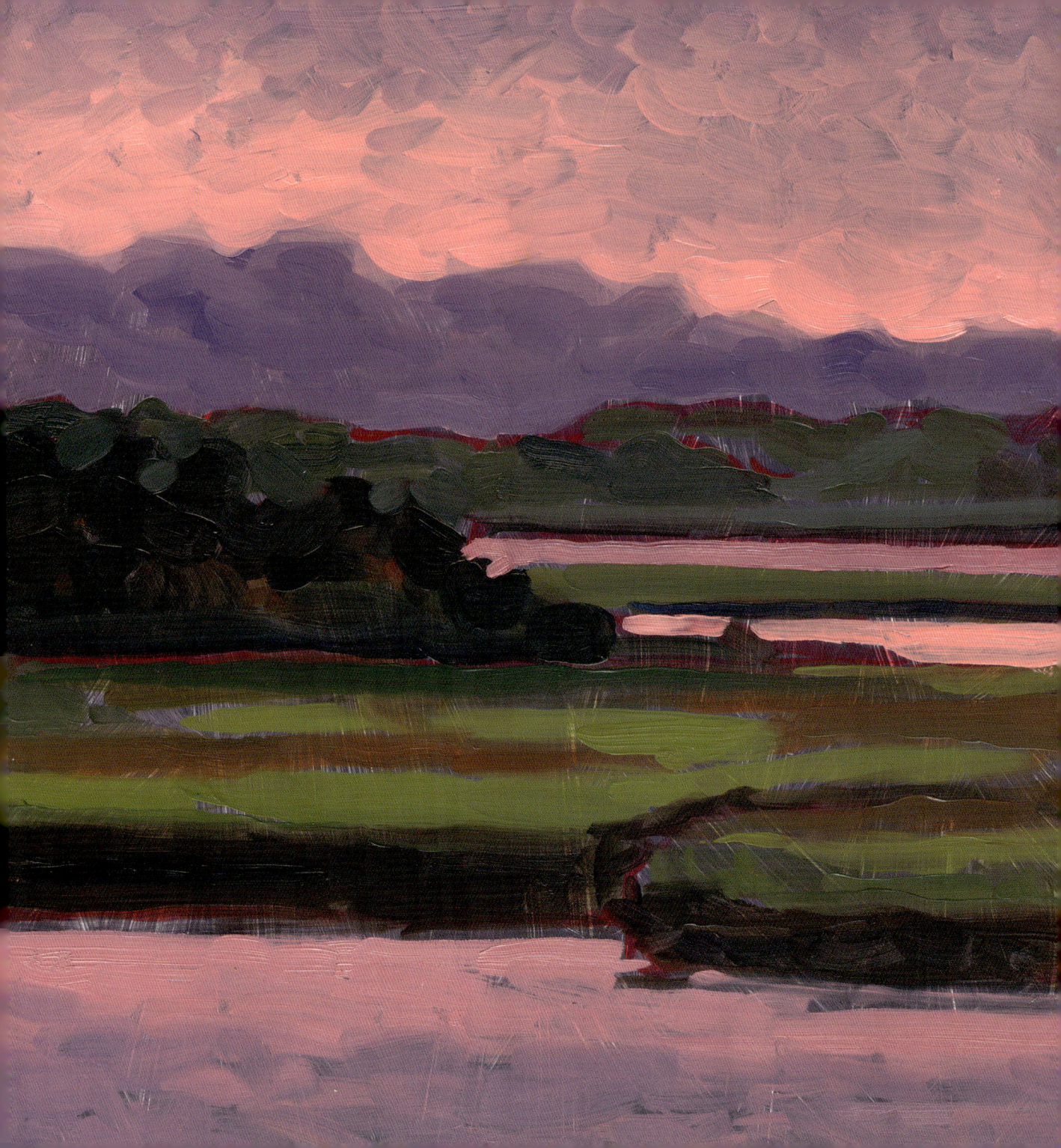

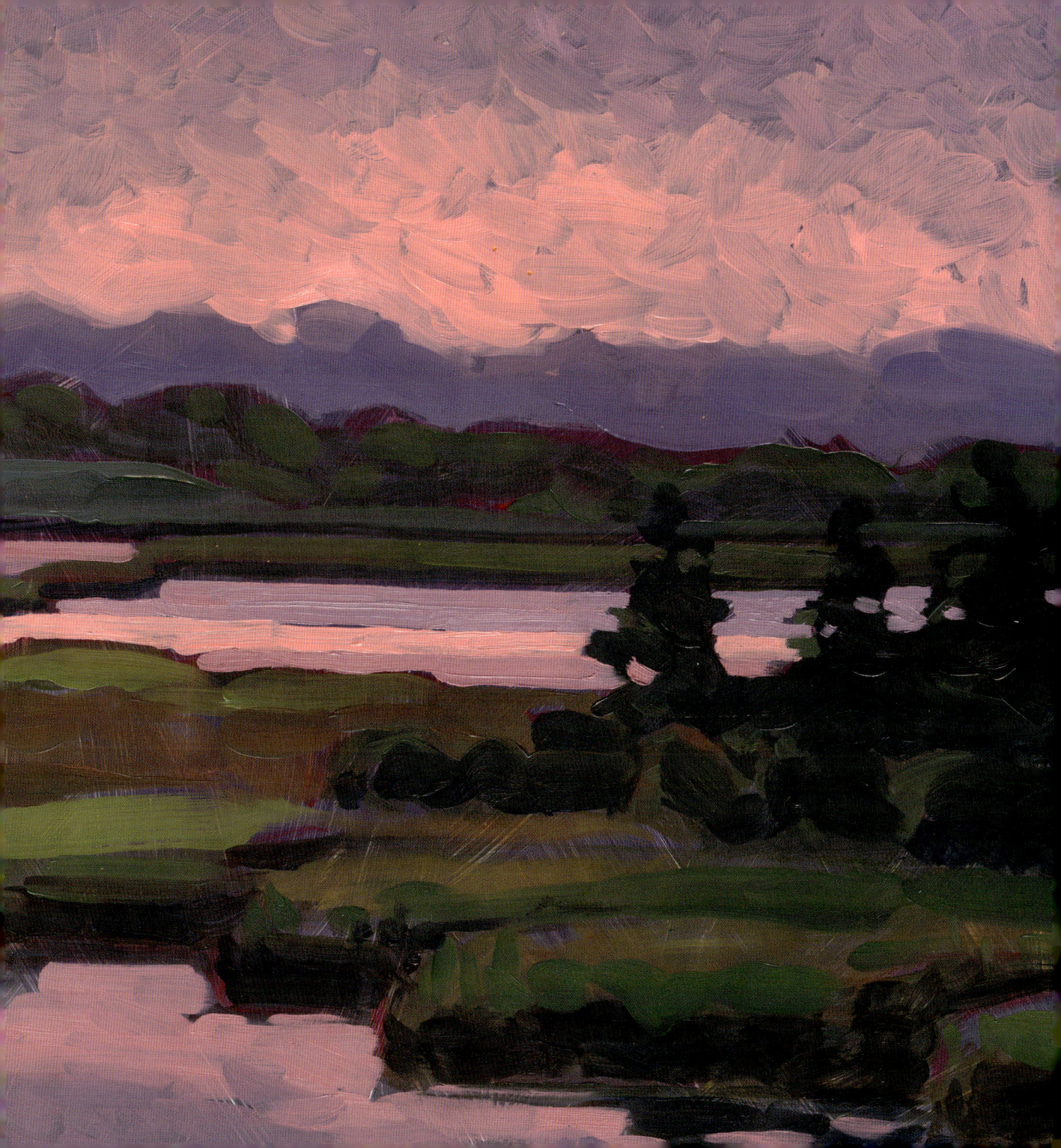

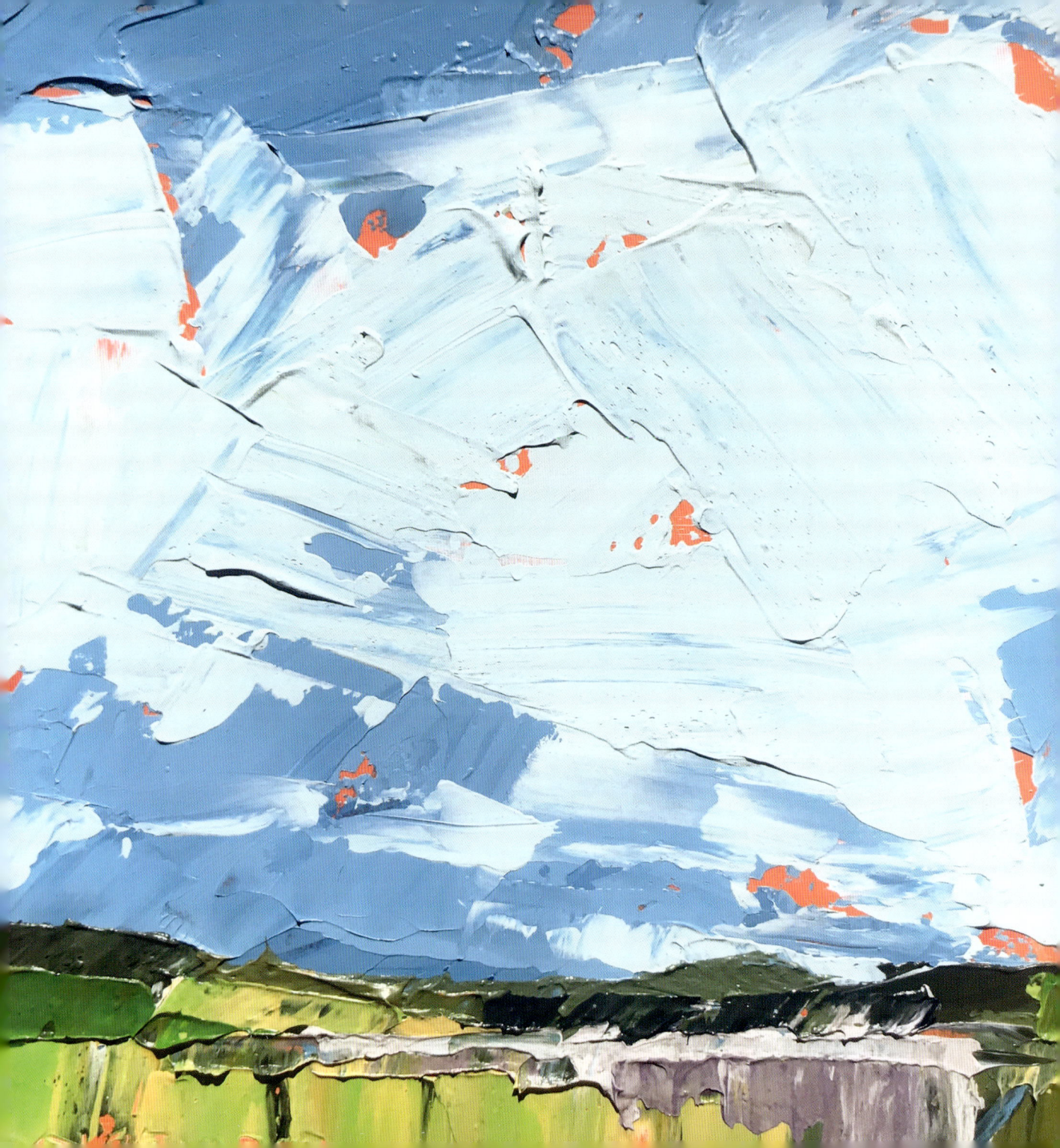

First Island Corn

We rise with the jays
pack the trunk with an empty cooler
a towel for the inevitable swim.
Drop the top
press play on the mixtape
head up island.

Rolling green hills
ancient stone walls
lacy beetlebung trees
cows and chickens
goats and geese
alpaca too.

Farm after farm
of plump summer squash
fresh chops
aged cheddar
fragrant tarragon
just-laid eggs.

At last, fields of gold.
Eureka.

Honor System

The unmanned roadside flower stand is a Vineyard staple.
They're scattered about the Island—bouquets of pinks, reds, purples
standing proudly in mason jars next to a small wooden collection box
and a hand-painted sign, *Flowers $10*.

Folks from away can't always fathom it: Why do locals trust
each other to do the right thing and open their wallets?
Of course, some of it is geography. On an island, there are only
two ways off—and the third is to swim. Makes you think twice.

But it's also just a *we're-all-in-this-together* kind of thing. Islanders are
of the same tribe. And in a tribe, making off with a bunch of
your neighbor's flowers violates the code.

At the flower stand, no one sees the transaction and there's no gold star
for participation. But every time a bouquet is picked, a $10 bill drops
into the wooden box. Often with an extra fiver for good measure.

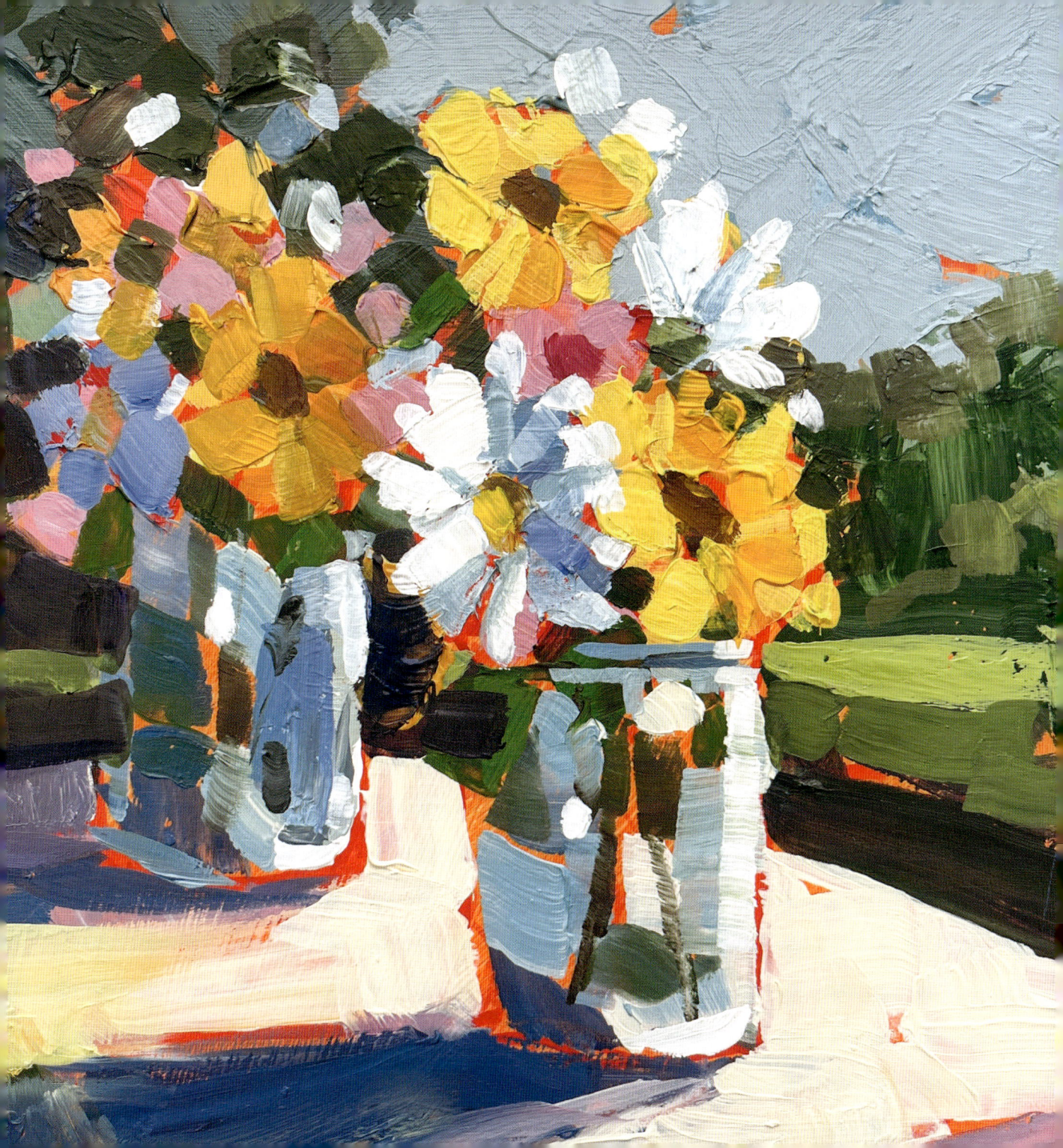

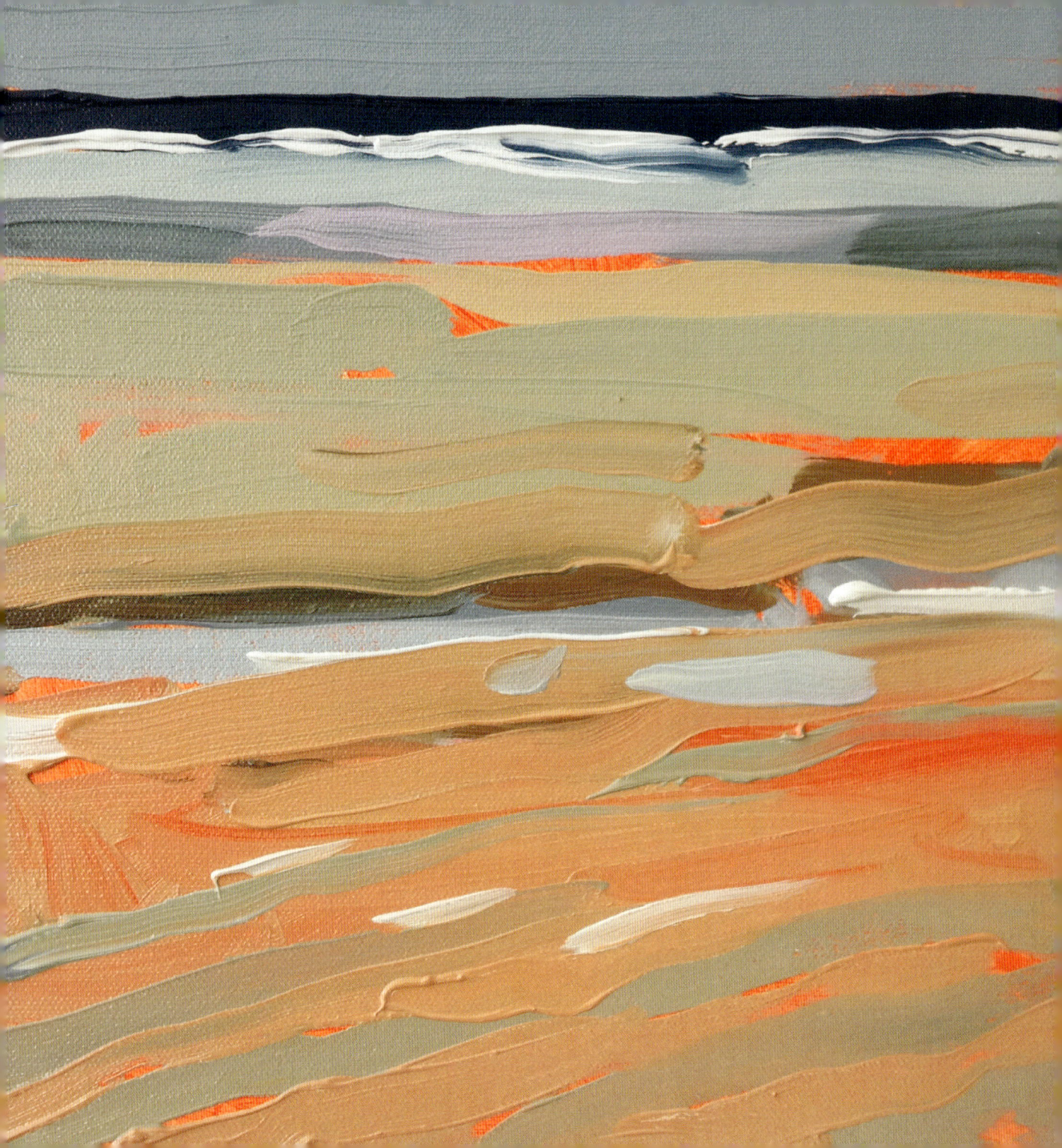

Water Color

pigment clings

to eddy's edge

tide ebbs

as pools dry

ochre and cobalt

remain true

in the end

Raw Bar

The Vineyard is known well for its sweeping ocean vistas,
picture postcard hamlets, white fences and blue hydrangeas.
Its pastoral scenes and thriving agricultural community,
decidedly less so. And yet this 87-square-miles is home to
dozens of farms and a network of nonprofits connecting
year-round residents to a near-constant flow
of seasonal meats and cheeses, fruits and vegetables.

This summer, the early yield from our own porch pot is
small but promising. Ripe and ready, each gives slightly
to the touch when picked, a juicy hue previewing the sweet
succulence inside. We could toss them into a bowl with
some burrata and basil or patiently wait for them to blister
on the grill. But instead we stand at the kitchen counter
and greedily gobble them up, vine to mouth.

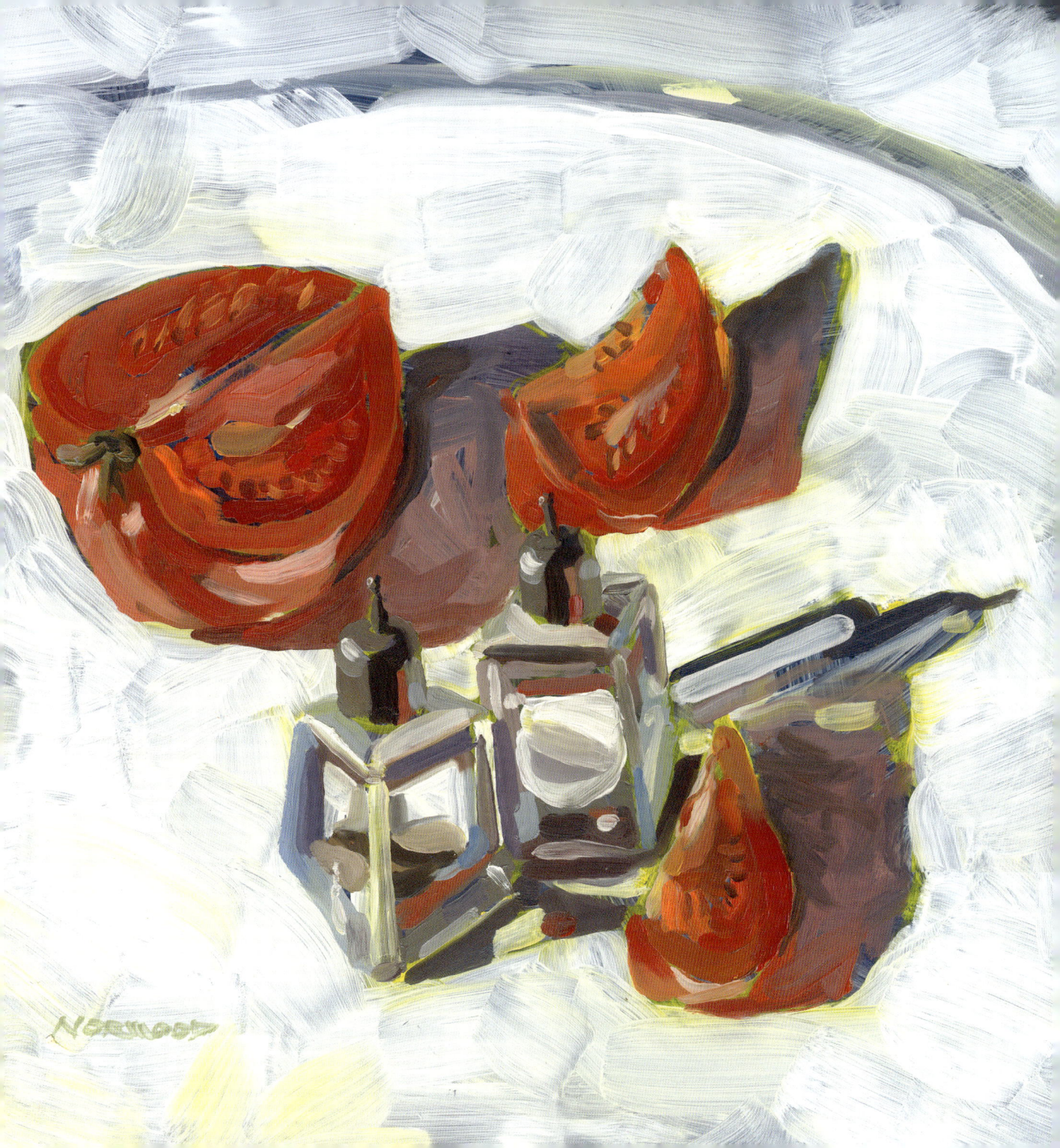

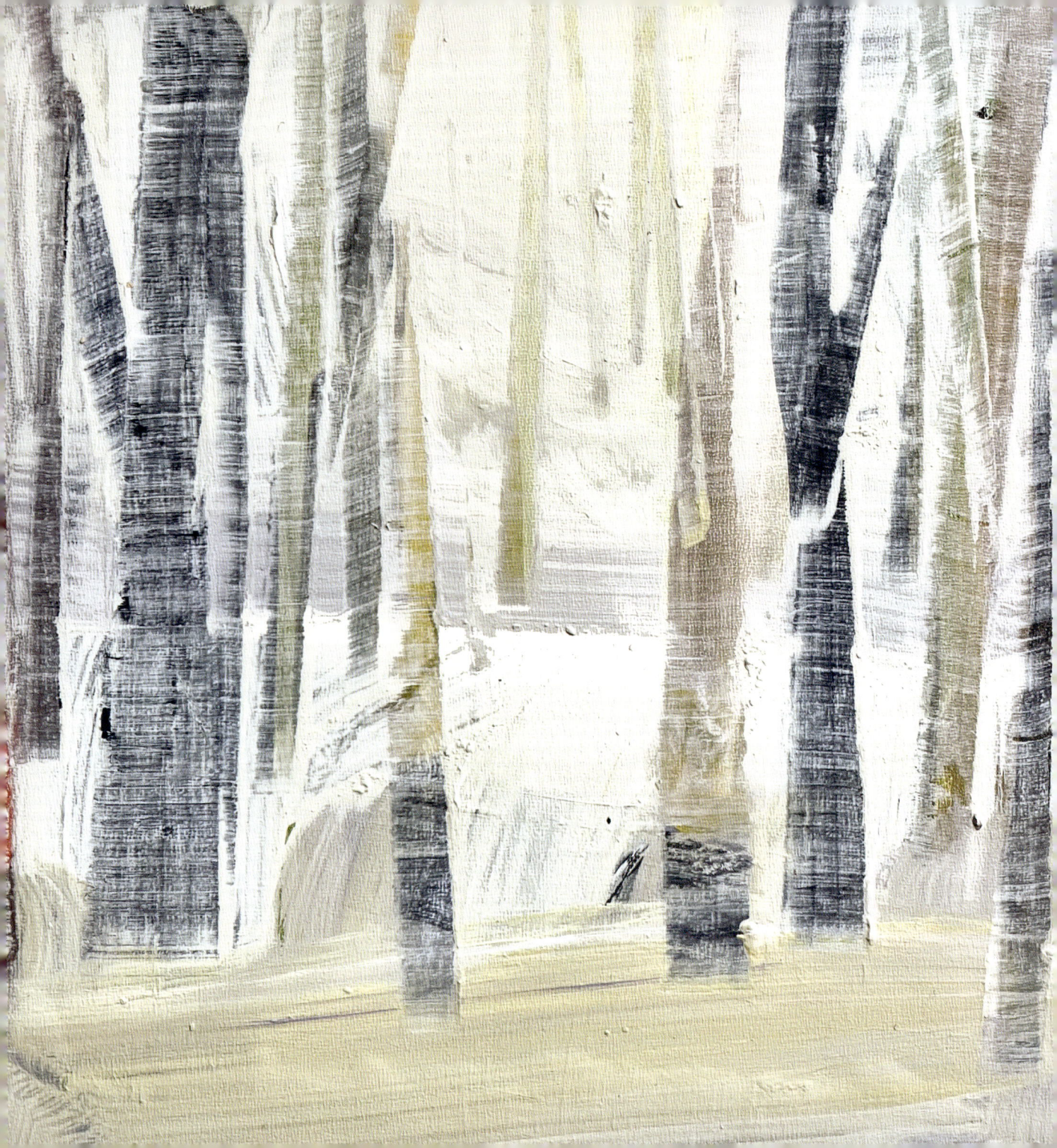

Moonshadow

In these wee hours
not a soul on the endless stretch
between Oak Bluffs and Edgartown,
flooded by a luminous moon
like an old movie shot day-for-night.

We kill the headlights for a few seconds
risking a run-in with the cops
or worse, a wandering deer
but we're not worried:
tonight we are immortal.

As our eyes adjust
the scene emerges in photo negative
Sengekontacket Pond on one side
the Sound on the other
where the moon's twin ripples milky
in the black sky.

A thick silence envelops us
at once comforting and unsettling.
We chicken out, flip the lights back on.
The snapshot recedes,
etched in our minds
like the fleeting green flash of a sunset.

Beach Key

"South Beach" typically refers to the stretch of sand between the forks
off Katama Road, which in summer becomes an endless quilting of towels
and coolers and umbrellas.

In reality, south beach stretches the entire length of the southern edge
of the Island and goes by many different names: Norton Point, Long Point,
Sepiessa, Quansoo, Lucy Vincent, Windy Gates, Squibnocket, Philbin.

Sometimes, when solitude calls out, we make a game of finagling our way
onto these private "unreachable" beaches, to dodge the crowds and see the sea.

It takes some doing. We might need to borrow a 4x4, a kayak, a better map.
Locked gates, access stickers, and parking attendants sometimes stand in our way.

But every so often we succeed, finding ourselves on a blissfully empty expanse,
sharing it with no one but the occasional piping plover.

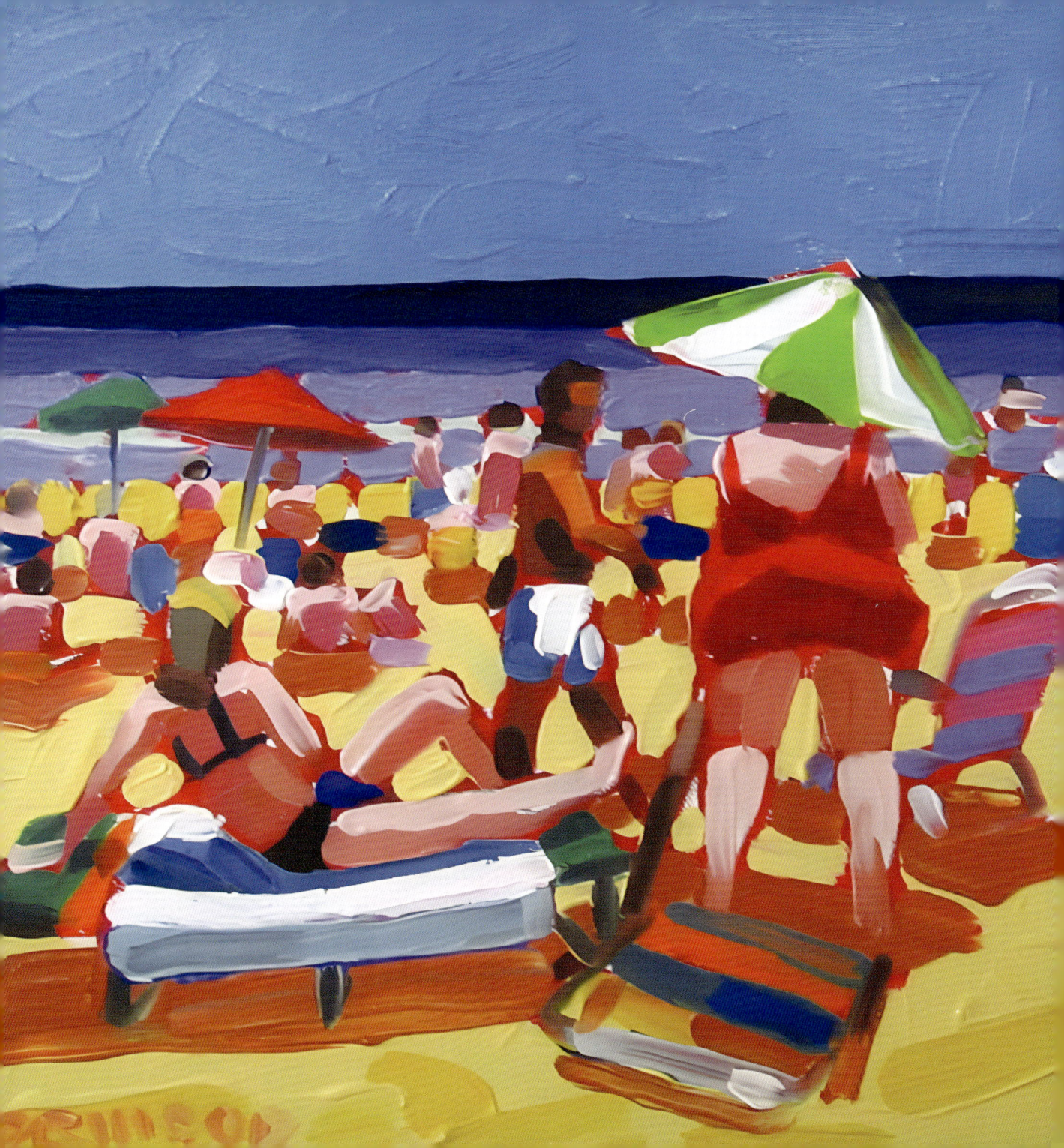

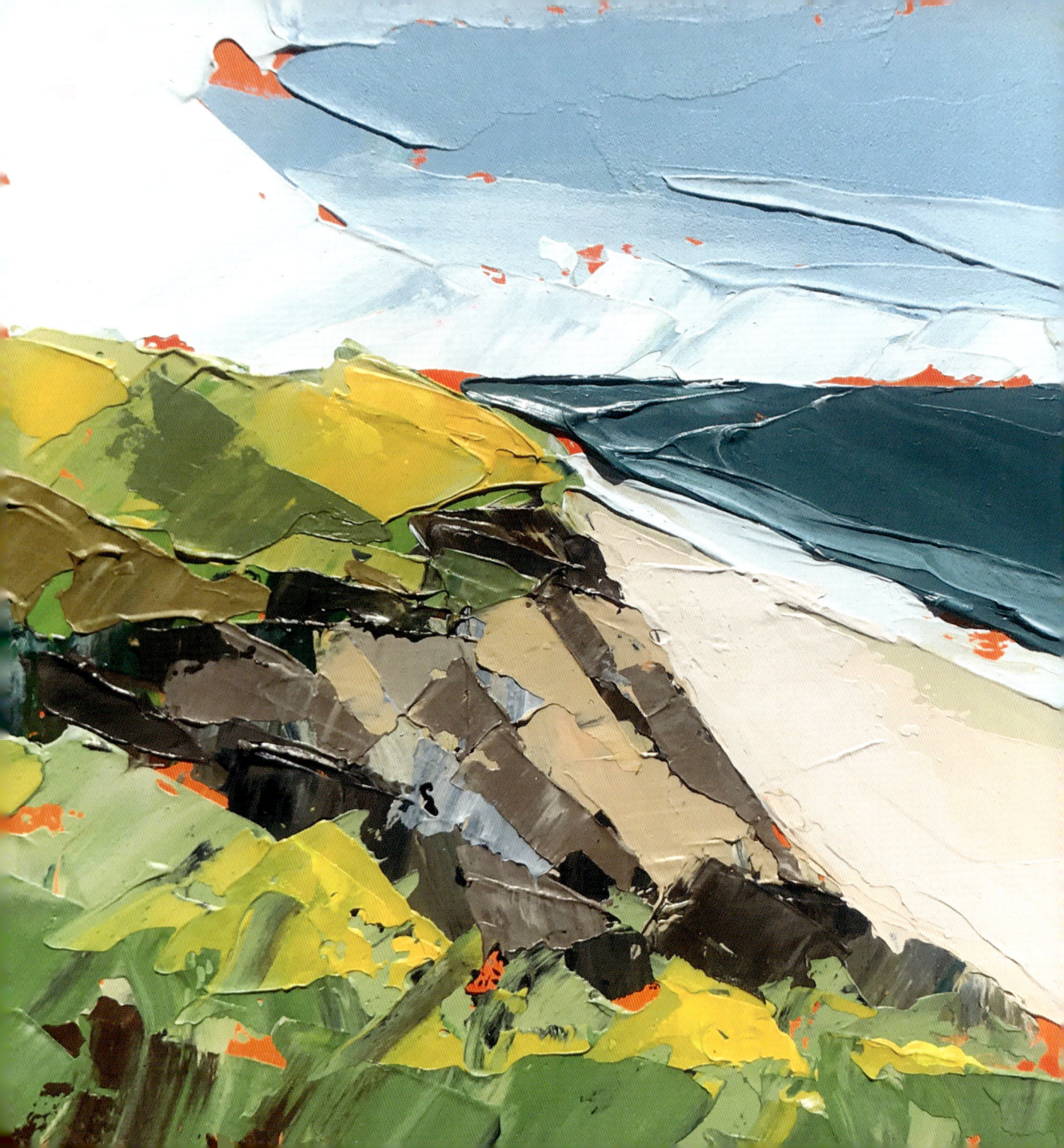

Moshup's Tale

He comes from the mainland
drags his colossal foot
plows through sand and sea.
This is how he makes Noepe.
He settles by the Aquinnah Cliffs
plucks plentiful whales from the sea
cooks them over eternal fire.

Years upon years
layer upon layer
recorded in rock.
Whale bone
seal skin
shark teeth
quahog shell
petrified wood
burnt ash
fire clay
tribal dreams.

Chasing Waves

it's a never-ending race
back and forth
in and out
swift
urgent
dizzying
like the sprint
of summer
itself

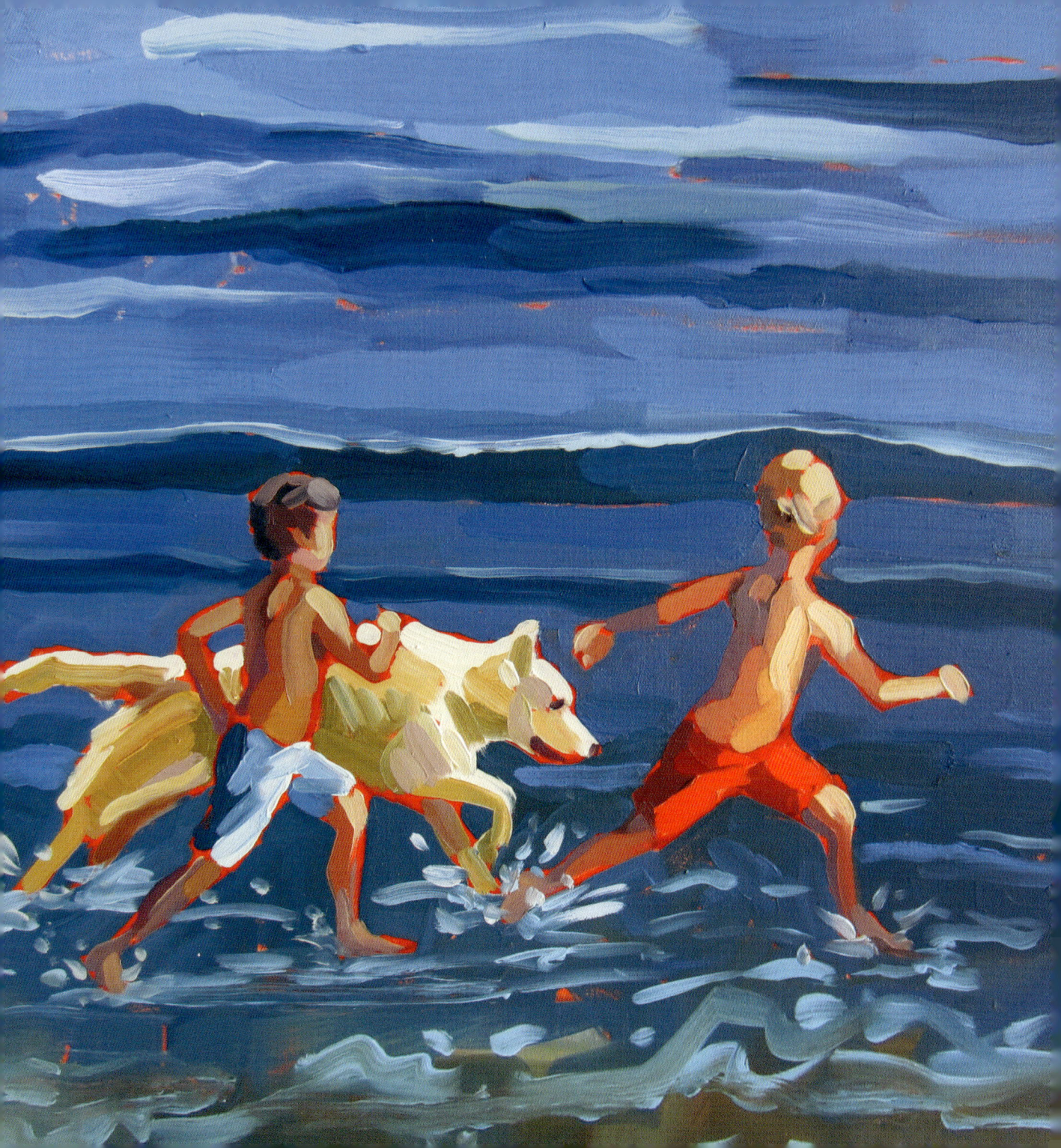

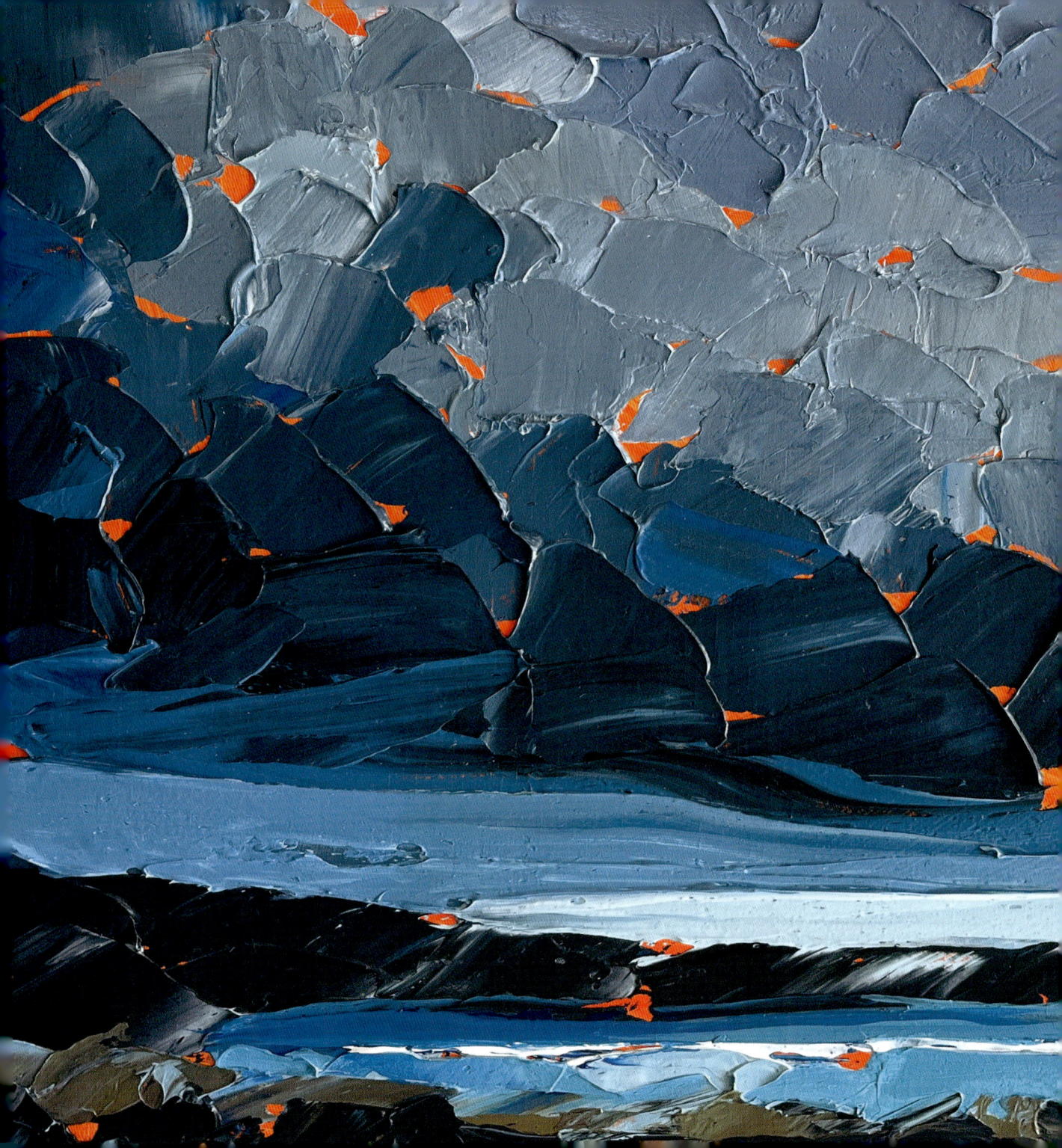

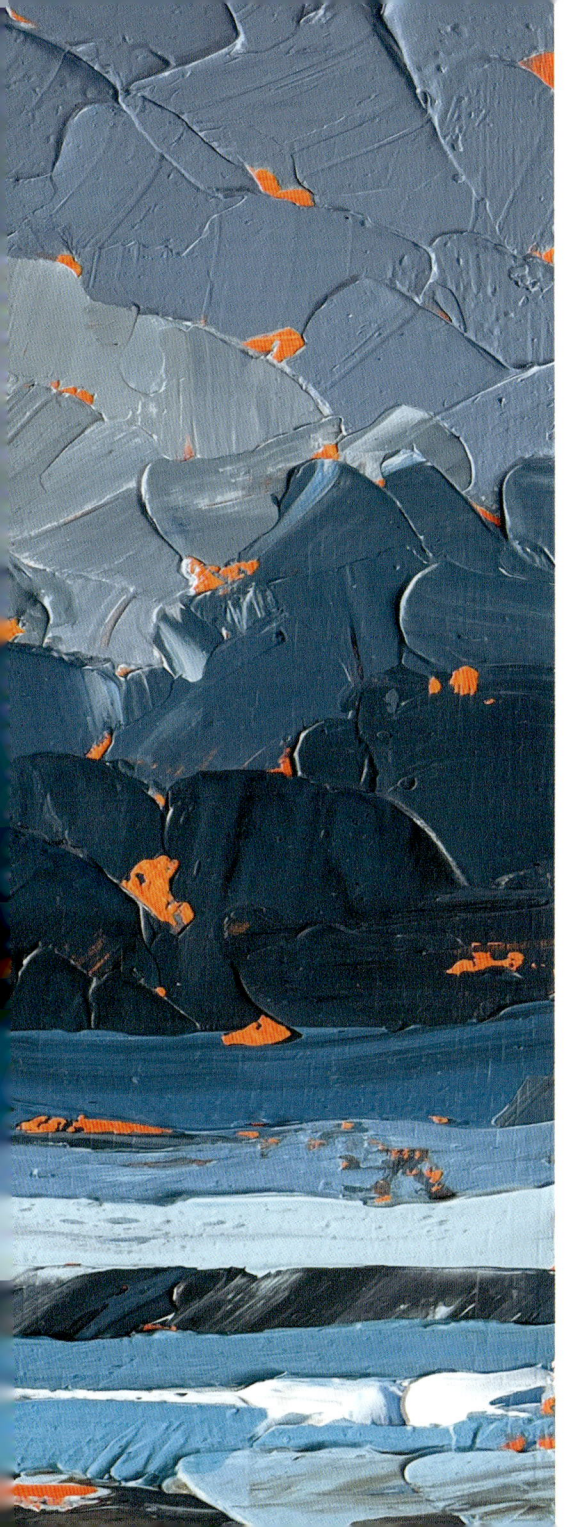

After Hours

we wake from sandy sleep, half
past midnight, midsummer, half
in the bag

fog blanket thick
fire long gone, no see ums
nipping at our ankles
beach blanket heavy with dew

we board our trusty skiff, point
the bow homeward, hug
the edges of the pond, read
the sharp eelgrass like braille

dim silhouettes and faint symphonies
of cicadas and night birds lead the way
and we reach the landing as the
sliver moon slices dawn

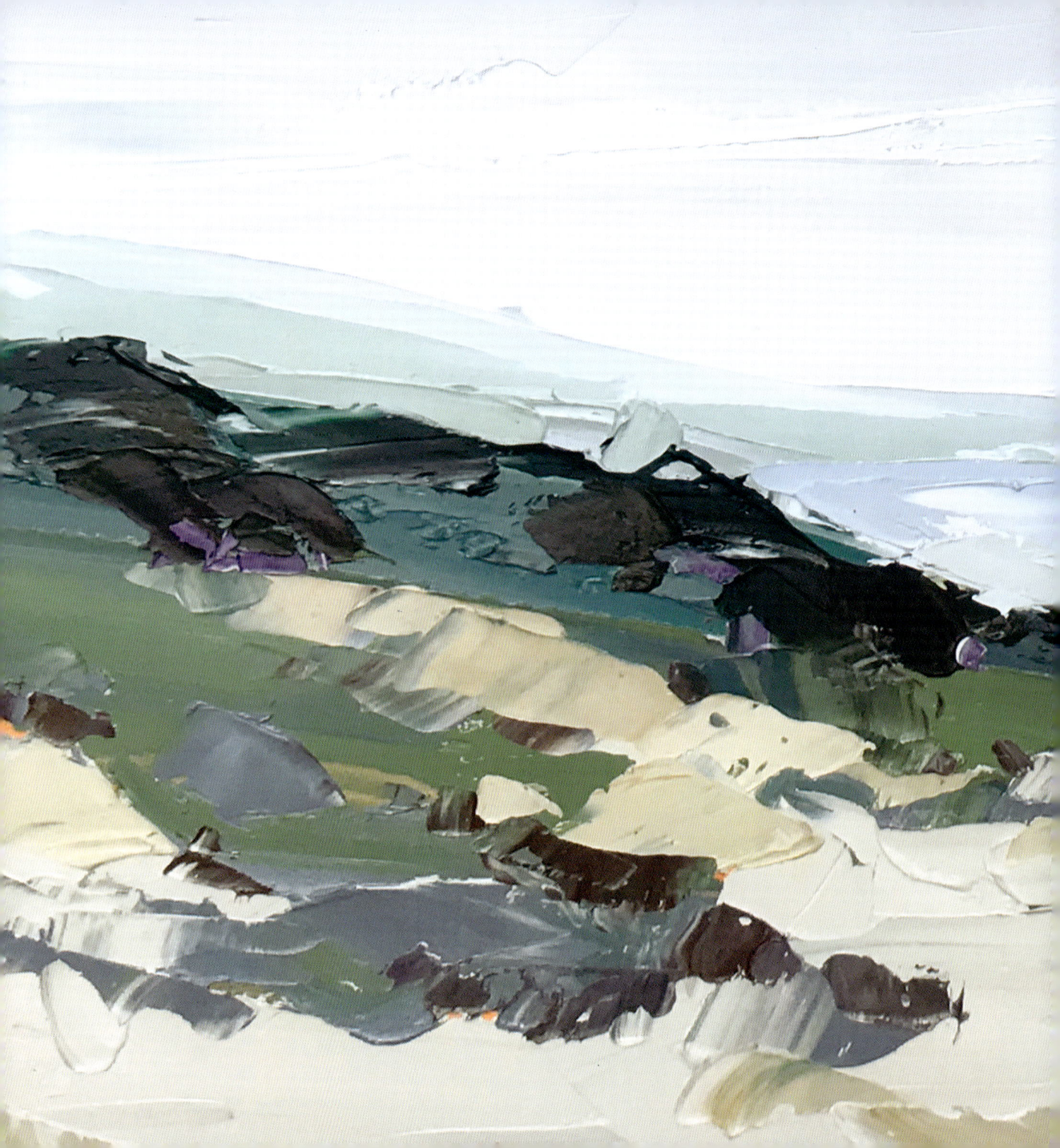

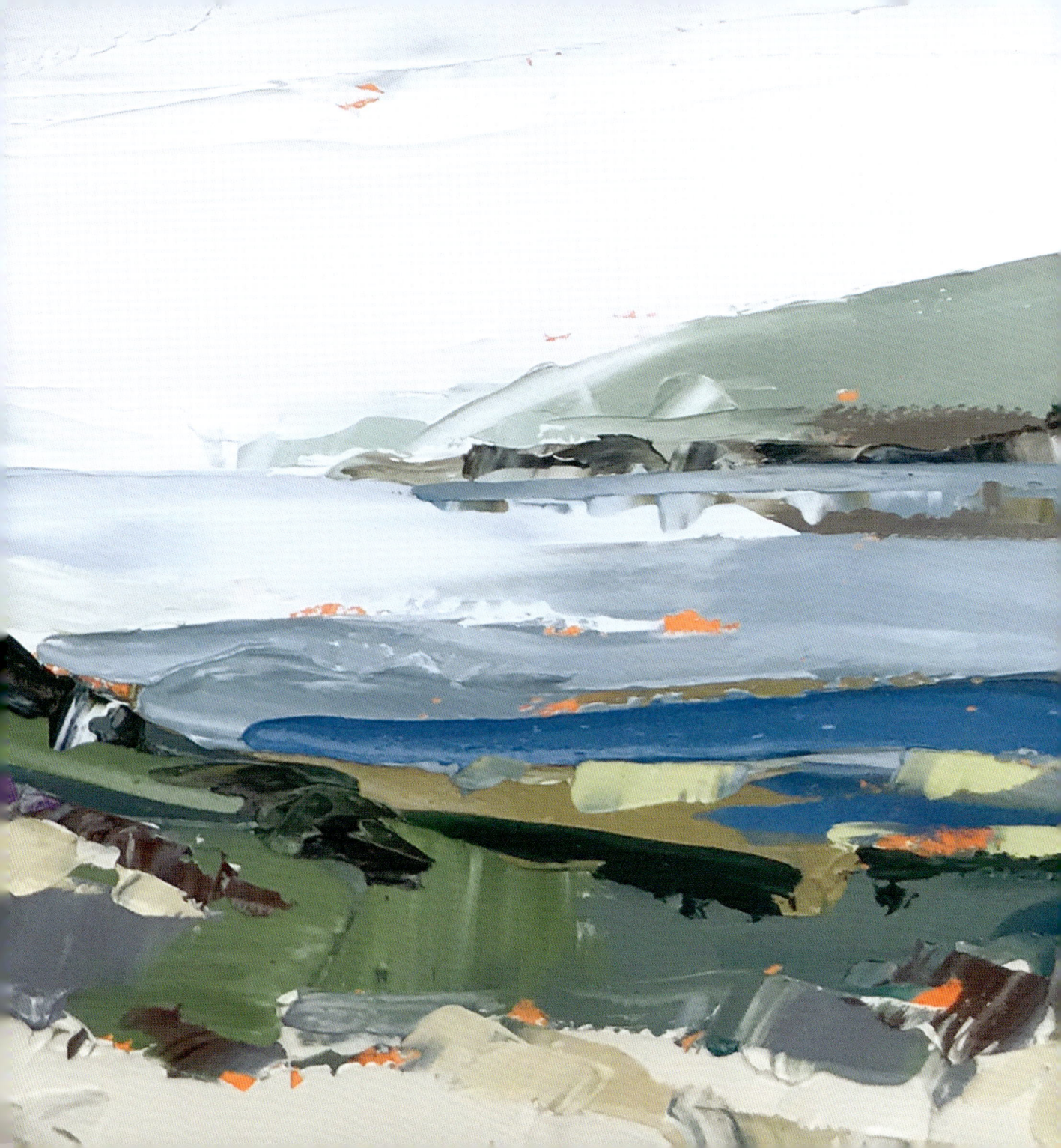

Cedar Tree Neck

Even in midsummer
when the island is sinking
under the swelling multitudes
there are places like this where
if we're lucky
we don't encounter another soul.

A handmade necklace of trails
loosely woven through the woods,
an exquisite pearl
waiting at the end.

In these noiseless refuges
we whisper
a word of thanks
to those who came before us
for tending this land
for those to come.

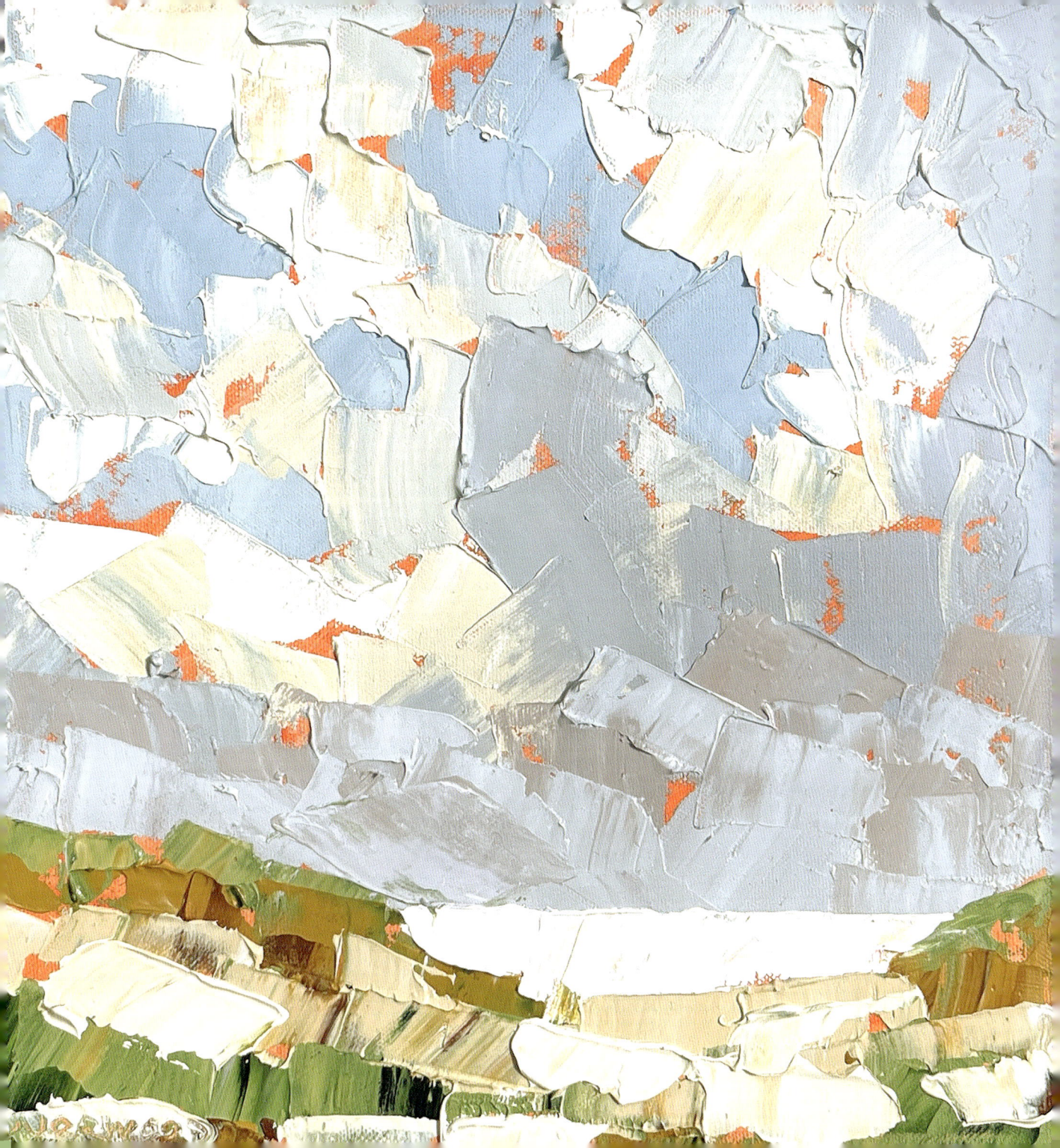

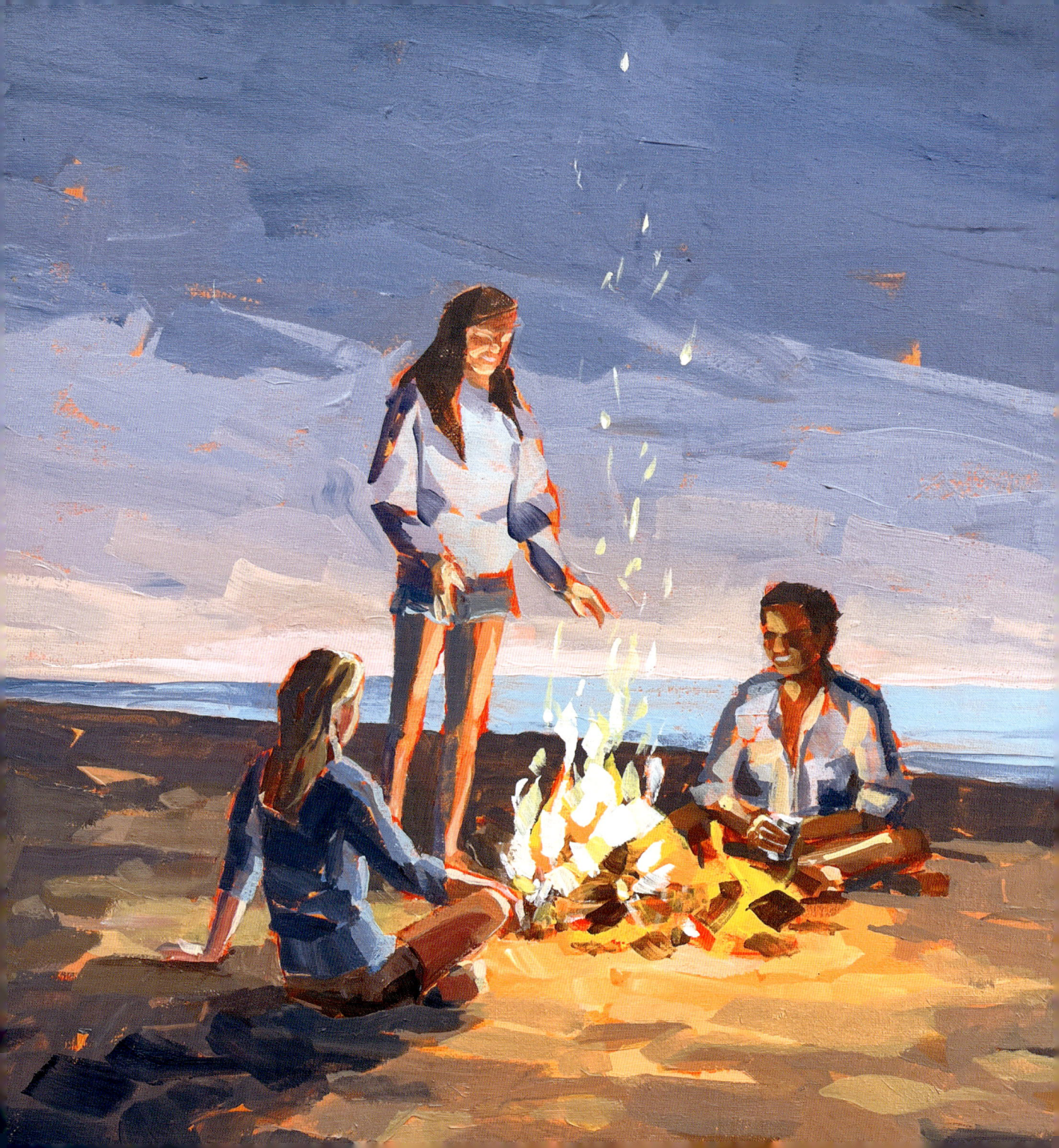

The Bonfire

At first only a few stars are visible as we click off our flashlights
but soon our pupils dilate and millions appear,
spilling from the Milky Way.

The air is damp and salty, our hair is wet
even though the sea spit us out hours ago.
We drop to our knees in the sand and begin to dig.

Sticks are arranged, newspaper is crumpled and shoved into the heart.
We stand up and take a breath, as if we've just built an entire seaside mansion.
Fish the lighter from the front pocket of beach-crusted jeans.

Click. Flick. The tiny flame teases the yellow paper of the Duraflame.
The damp sticks are oblivious. The newspaper is the first to succumb.
With a wink, the driftwood soon catches on.

We sit back in the sand to admire the orange dancing before us,
stinging our eyes and burning the soles of our bare feet.
Now is what we will look back on in the dead of winter.

Great Rock

How long did that glacier
take to saw through
millennia of ice and stone
to spit out this mammoth boulder
this lone rubble we sit atop
breathless from swimming and scaling
shins skinned, faces shining
waving to those ashore
less brave than we?

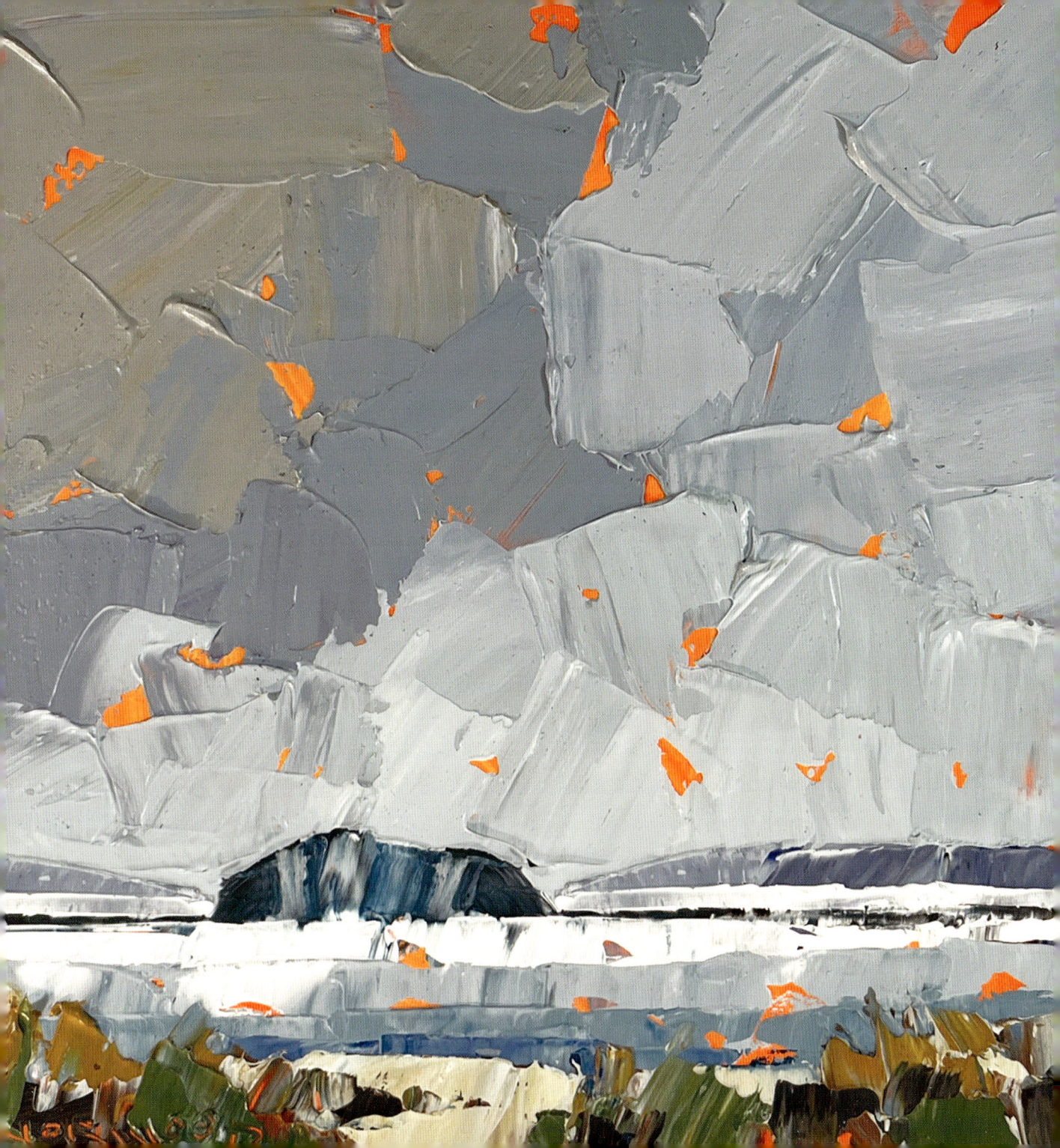

The Antidote

the best medicine
the cure for what ails
steep in saltwater
soak in the sun
soothe defuse dilute
evaporate into the ether
rinse

repeat

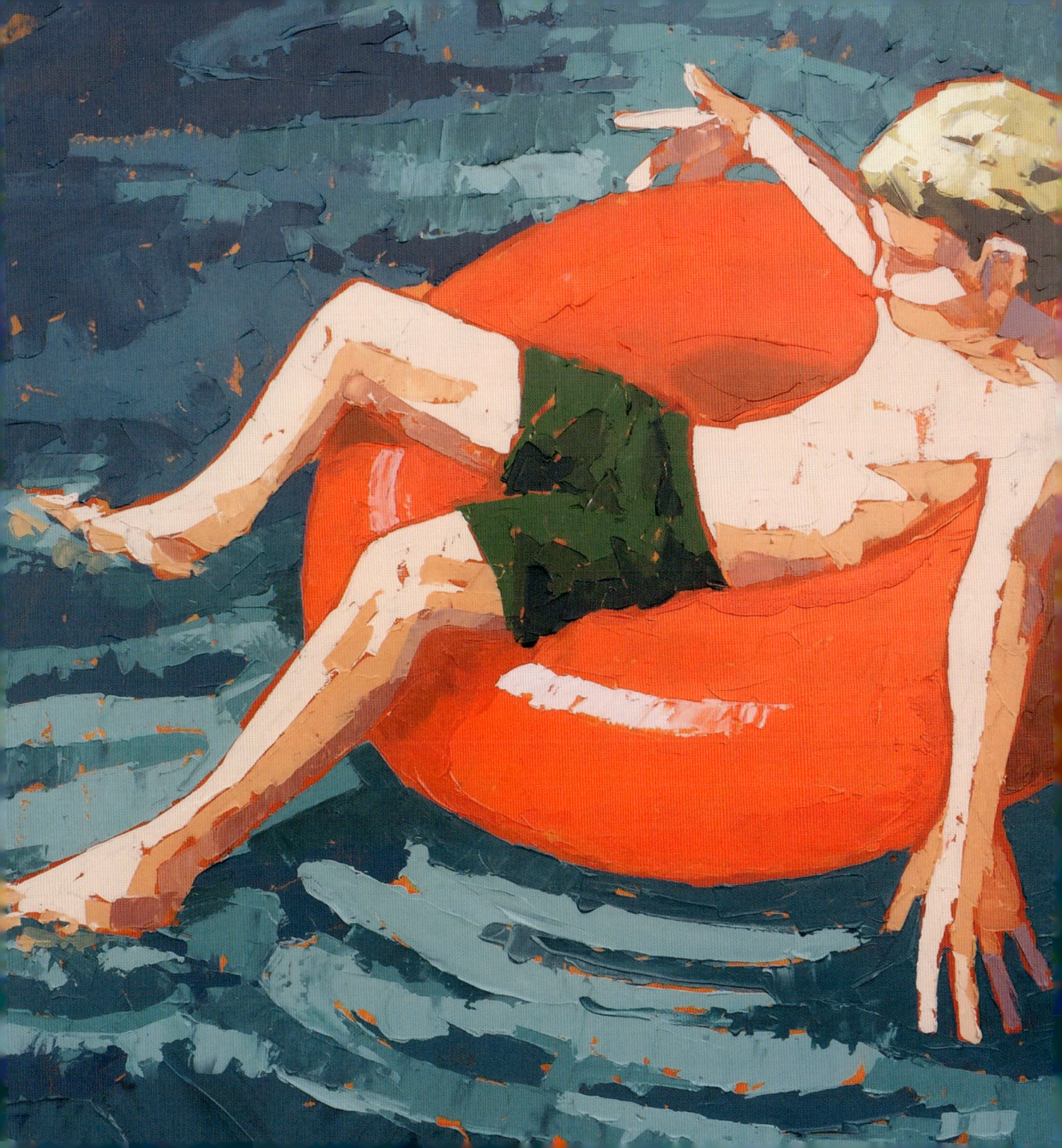

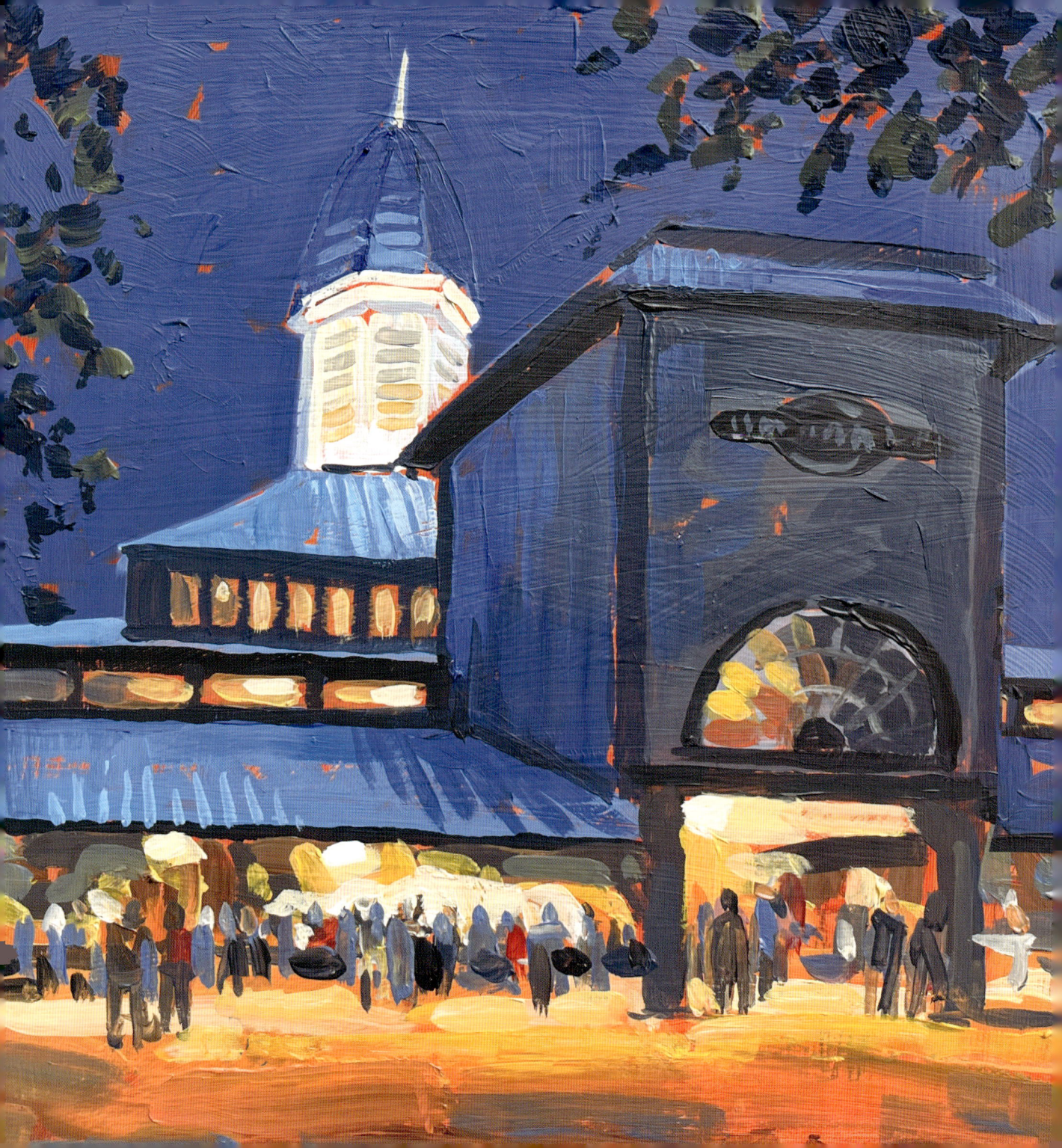

The Tabernacle

The first thing you notice is not
the Eiffel-style iron or the stained glass windows.

It's not the surrounding ancient oaks, candy-colored cottages
or swaths of lawn with kids playing about.

It's not the buzz of laughter, stories, and song spilling out
at all hours, day and evening.

The first thing you notice is there are no walls
No doors either.
No difference between what's in and what's out.

Just a great wide open, sweeping and generous
no matter who you are or why you've come
that says welcome, take a load off, stay awhile.

Elemental

every day
the same scenes
seem changed
feel new again

the breeze blows
from a different direction
the water molecules
and sand patterns shift
the quality of the light
from insistent to tender

our seeing is endlessly unfolding

can we ever really
know a place
if it never stops
surprising us?

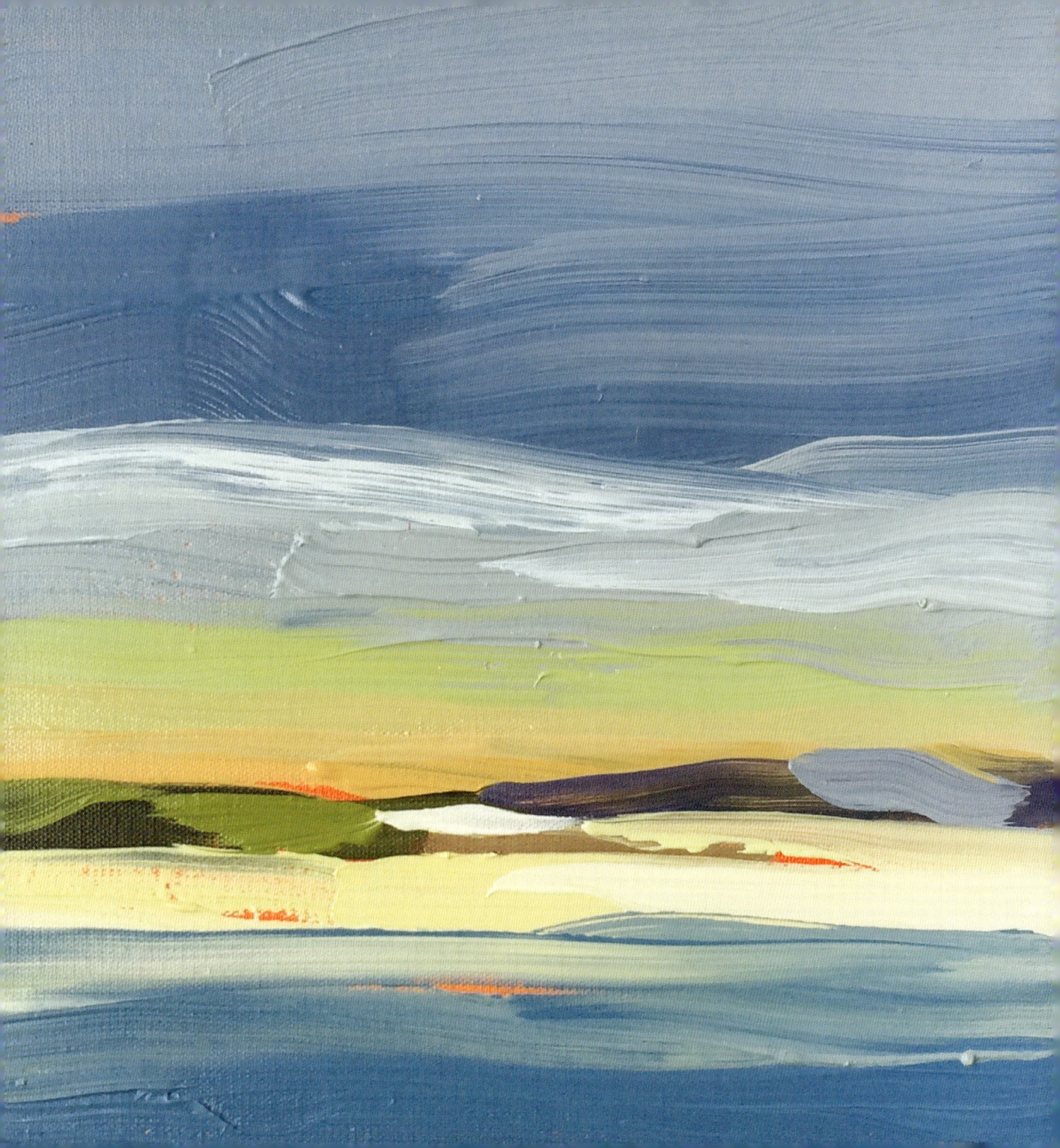

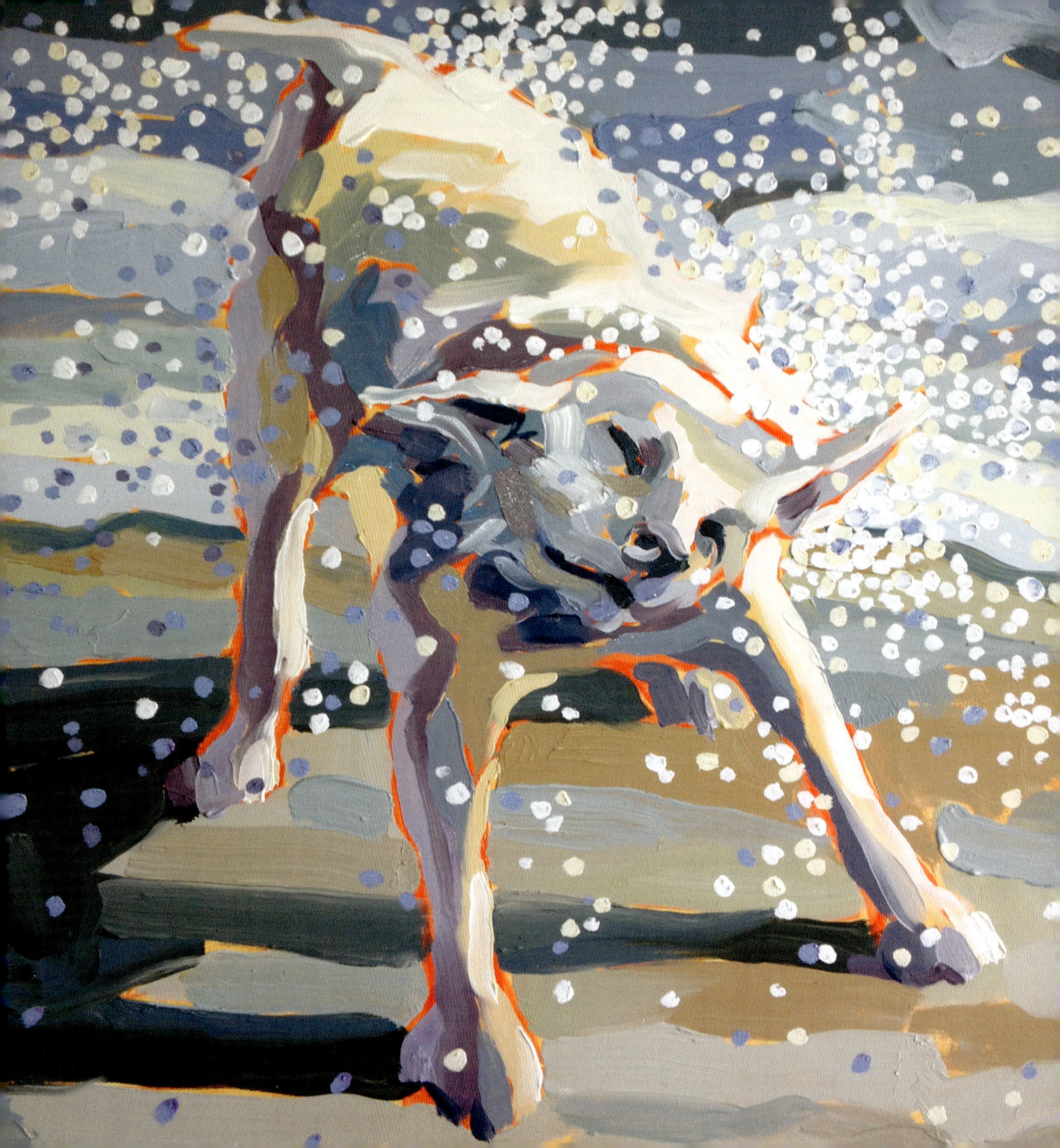

Summer Shower

The sky opens up
a sudden burst
to cool the skin
soak the scorching sand
rinse the dust off the scrub oak.

Before we can scamper for cover
or surrender to it
the clouds retreat
curtains parted
by the hand of the sun
signaling Act II
of a lazy beach afternoon.

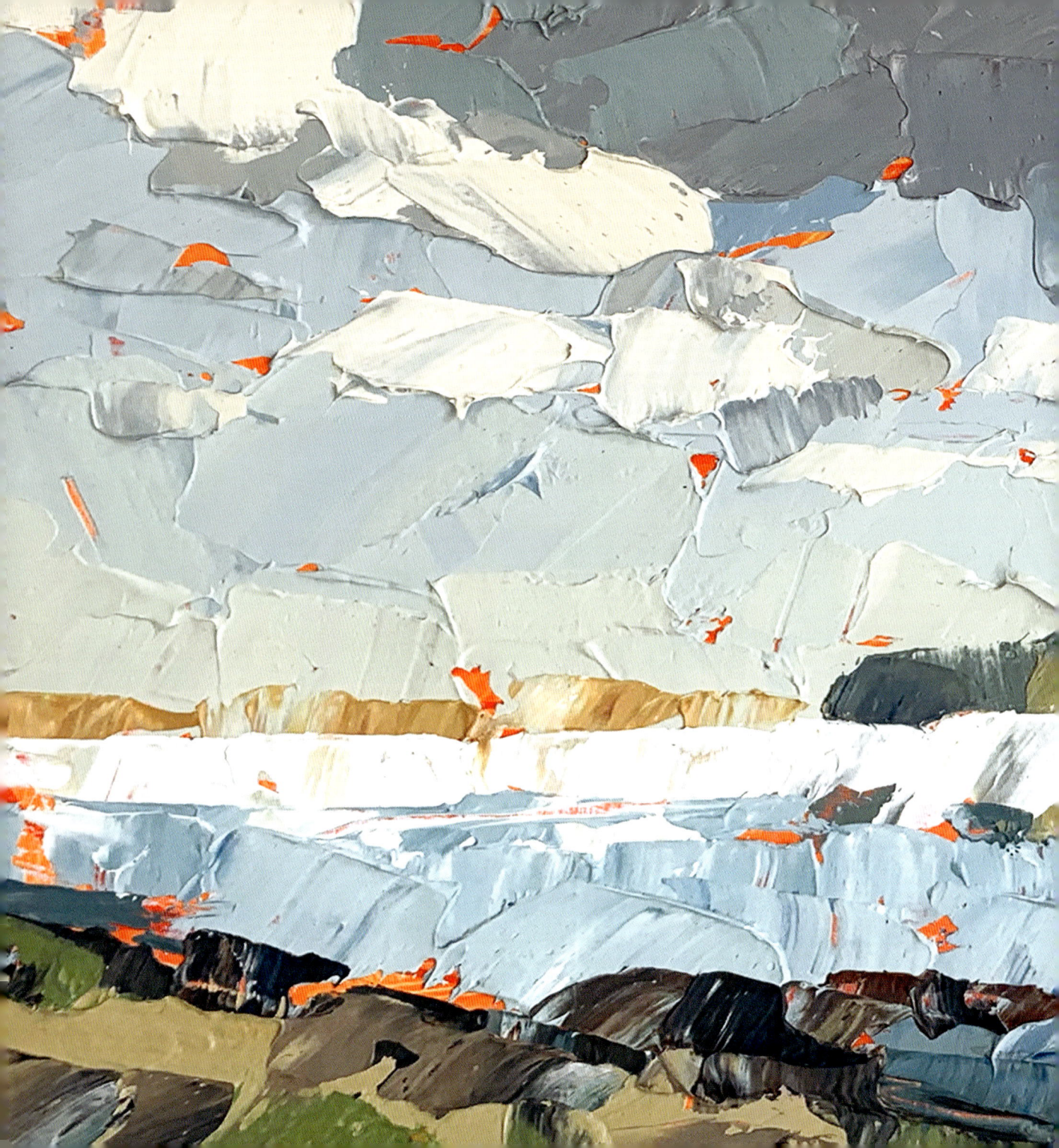

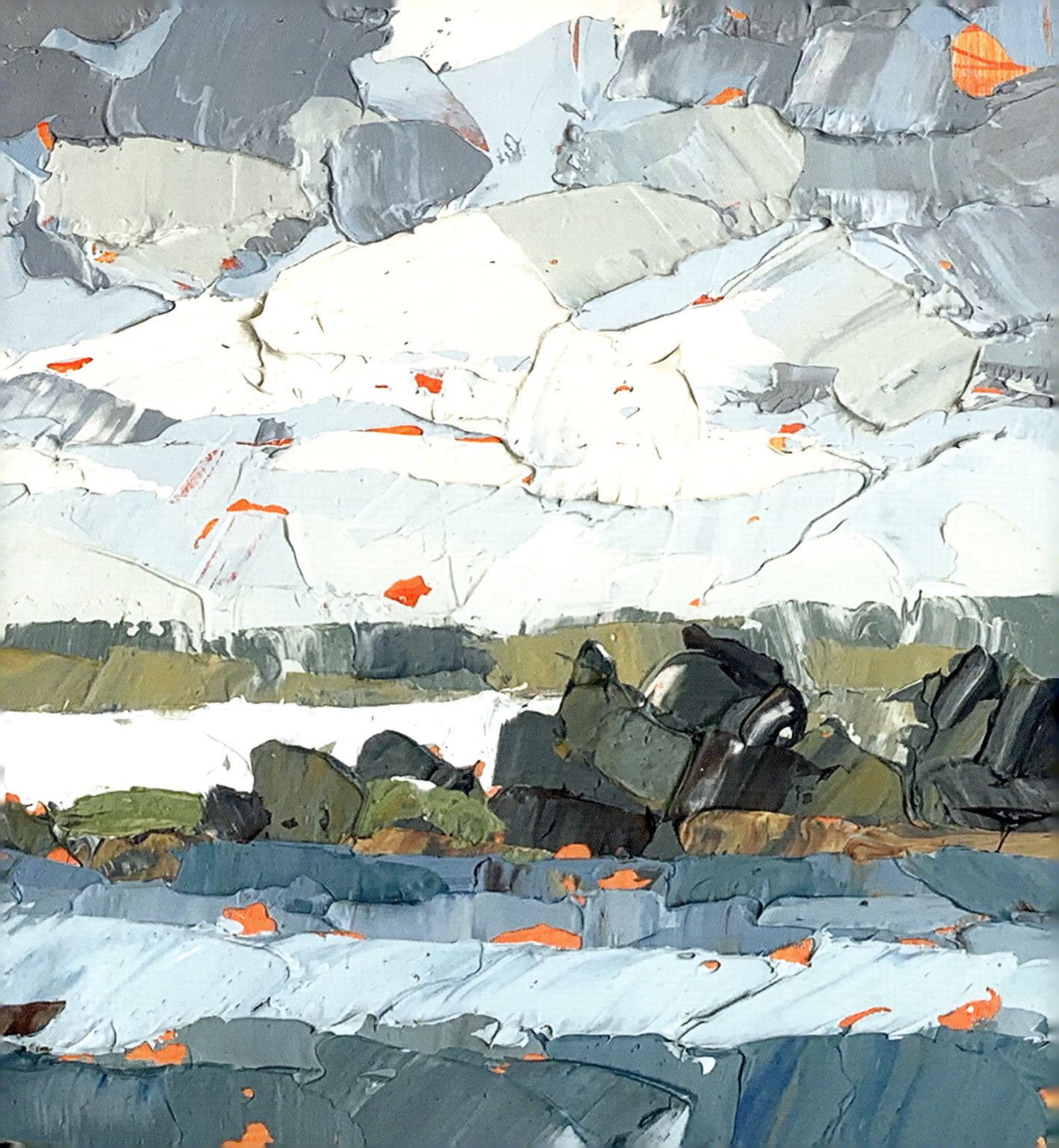

Chappy Ferries

They're not named *On Time II*
and *On Time III* for nothing.

Back and forth, rain or shine,
three cars at a time, a continuous loop
connecting the five hundred feet of harbor
between the busy village of Edgartown
and her sleepy sister Chappaquidick.

The ferries greet each other in the middle
like passersby on a narrow sidewalk, politely
stepping aside so the other can go around.

In high season, we prefer to
climb aboard on foot or two wheels.
Because when the car line backs up
ten and twenty deep
the ferry may be *on time*
but we most likely will not.

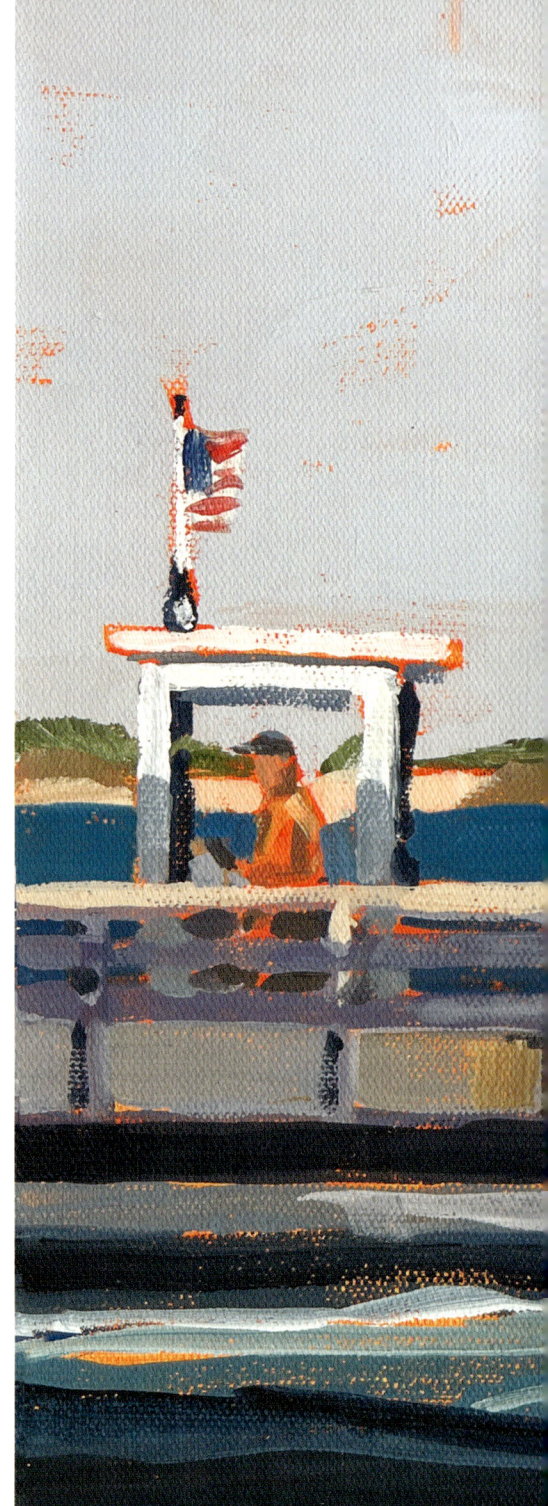

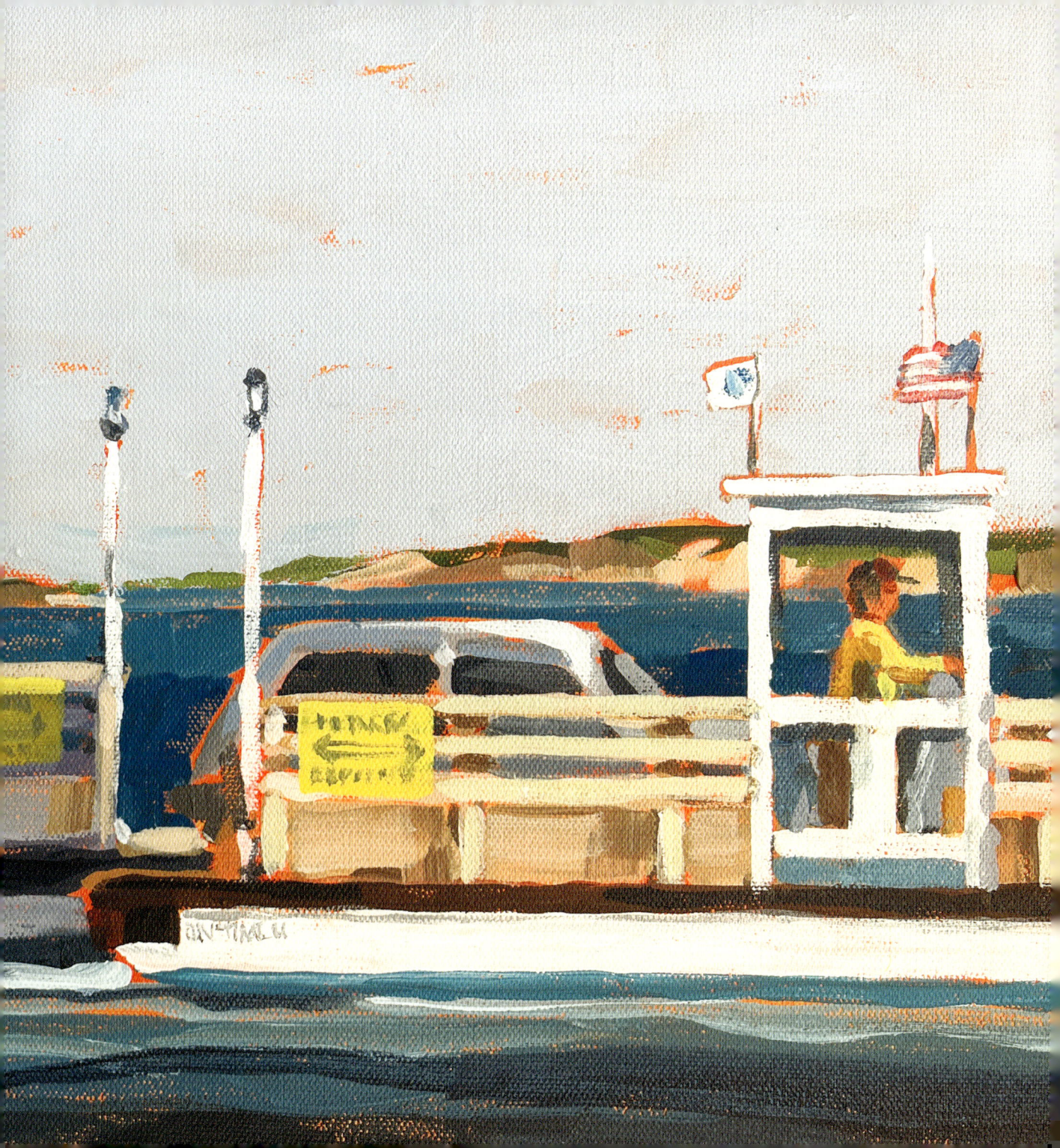

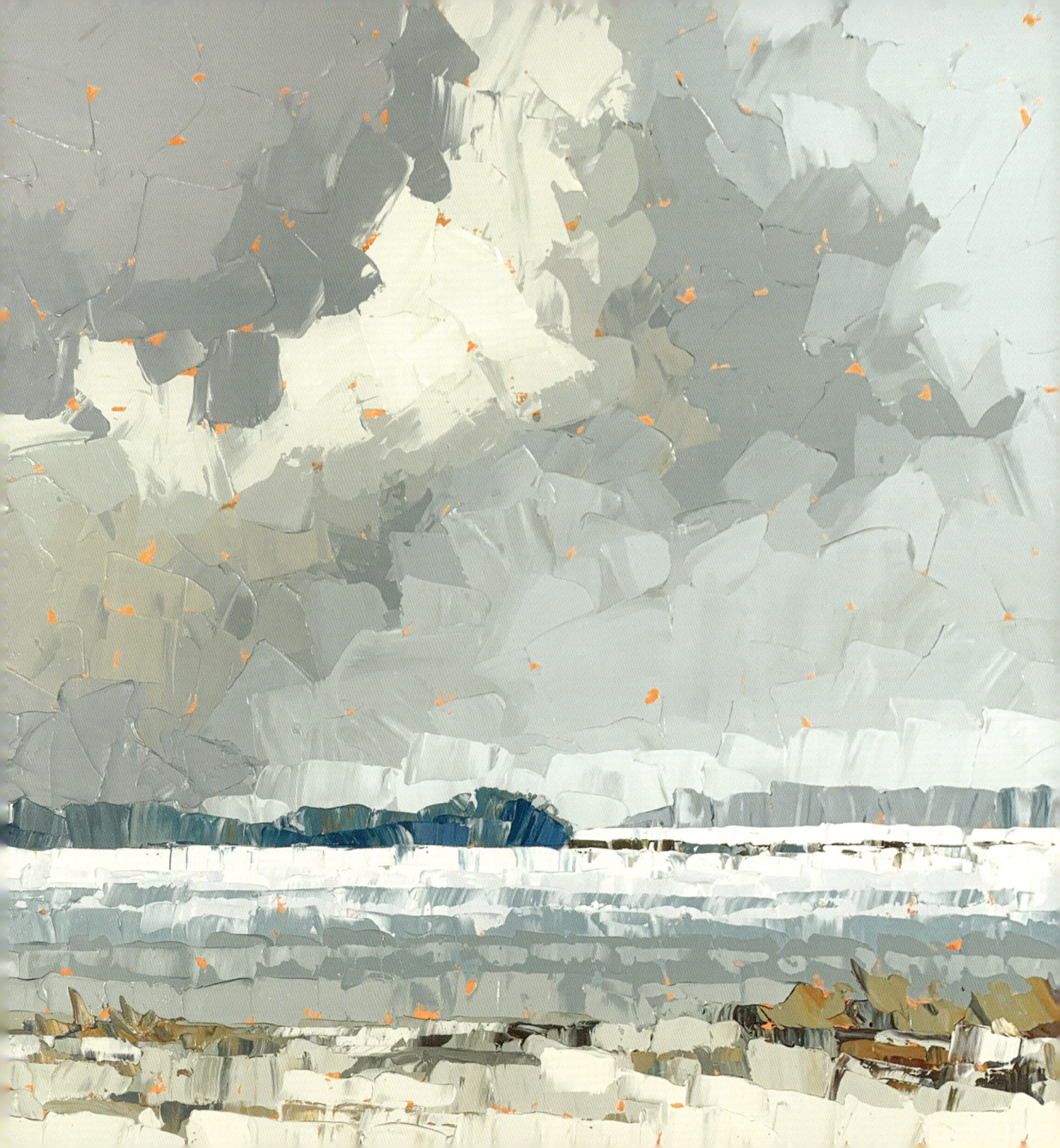

Quick Sand

summer shifts,

sifts

through a pinch of glass

through finger cracks

off into the waves

then back

again

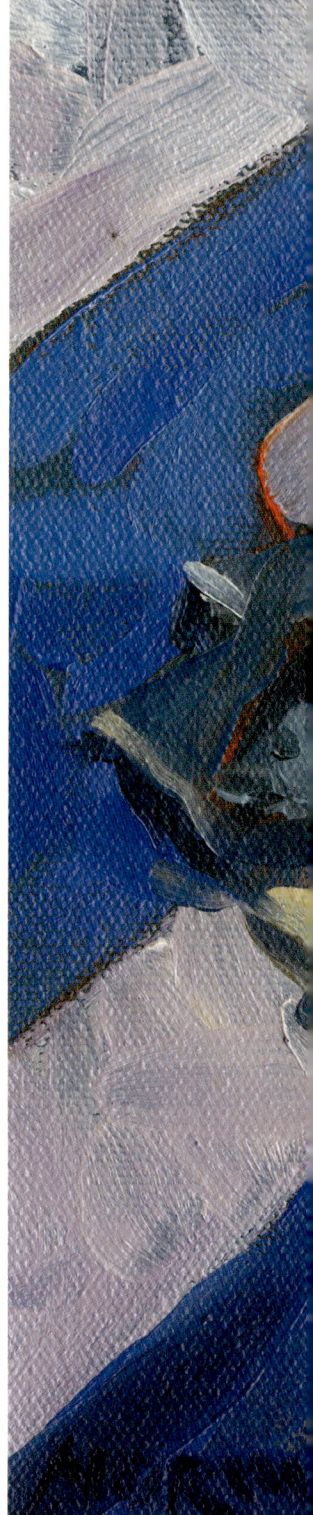

Smoked

The sea boils and bubbles
bluefish running bait fish
up the coast
onto the hooks
into the boats
one after another.
But they're just the warmup
for the real stars:
stripers, bonita, bigeyes.
Honored catch
that have no problem
getting into all the
high-season restaurants
we can't.

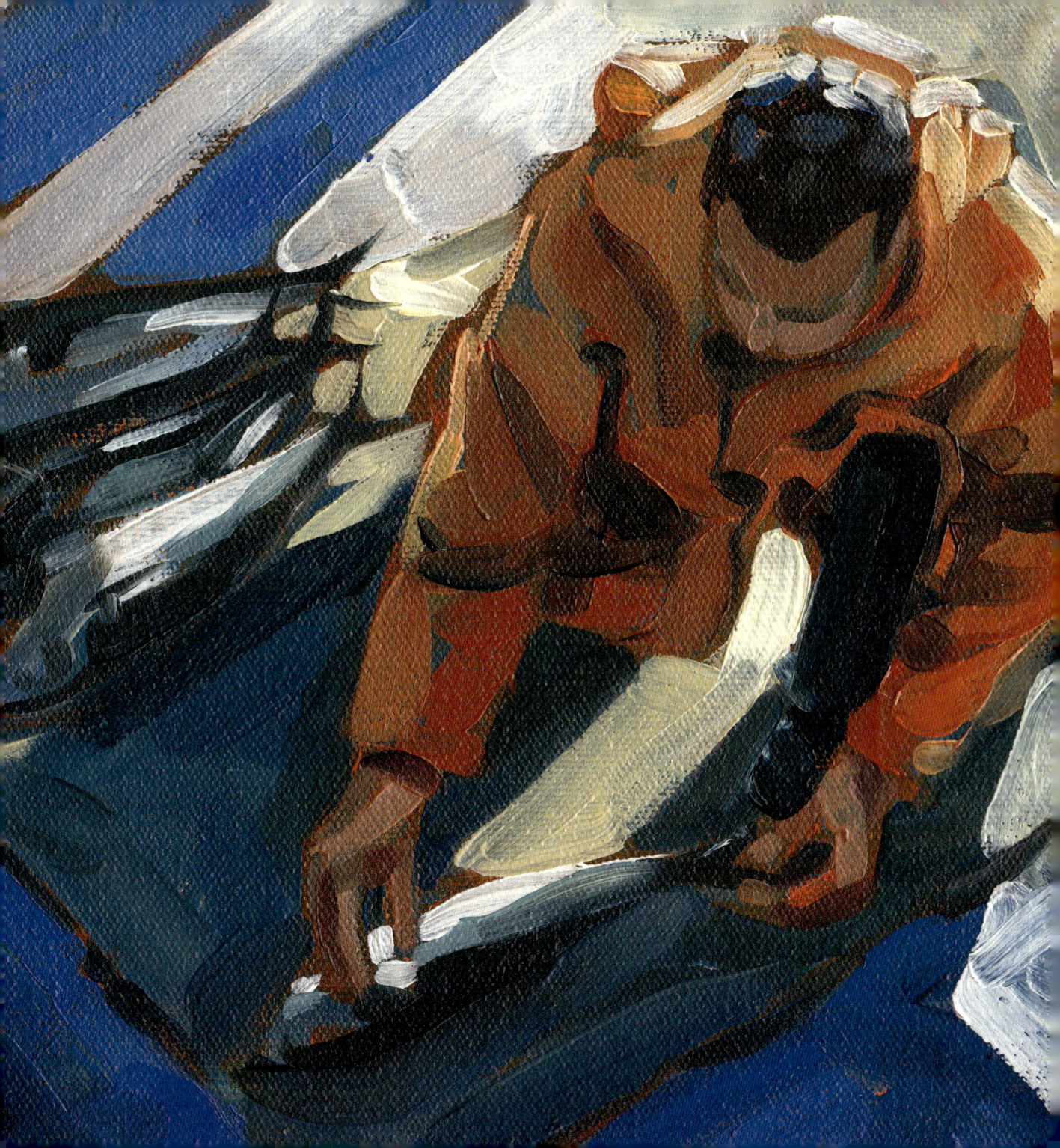

The Fair

Up here, from such great heights
we see as the birds do.
Even the clouds envy our lofty view
of the menagerie unfolding below.

The humming alpaca herd and the snuffling parade of oxen.
The dizzying teacups, tilt-a-whirl, and merry-go-round.
The twang of the bluegrass banjo, the clang of the skillet throw.
The warm waft of cotton candy and fried dough.

A temporary town risen from the soil
erected in a week, celebrated for four days,
dismantled in even fewer.

After the last apple pie is judged
and the show chickens re-cooped
all that remains is a scattering of trampled hay
a few kernels of kettle corn
and an open green field
fallow until next August
when the Ag Fair springs up anew.

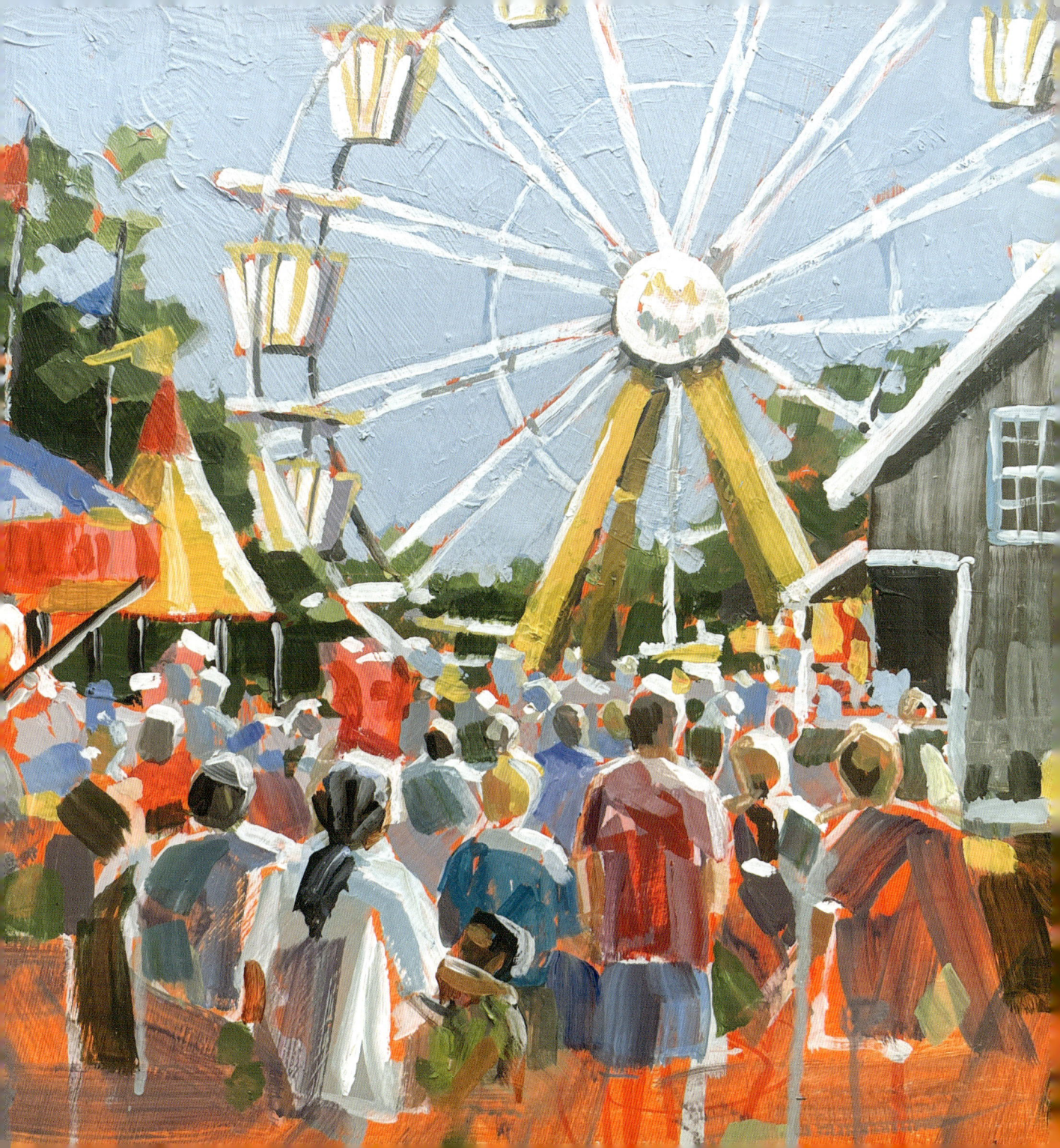

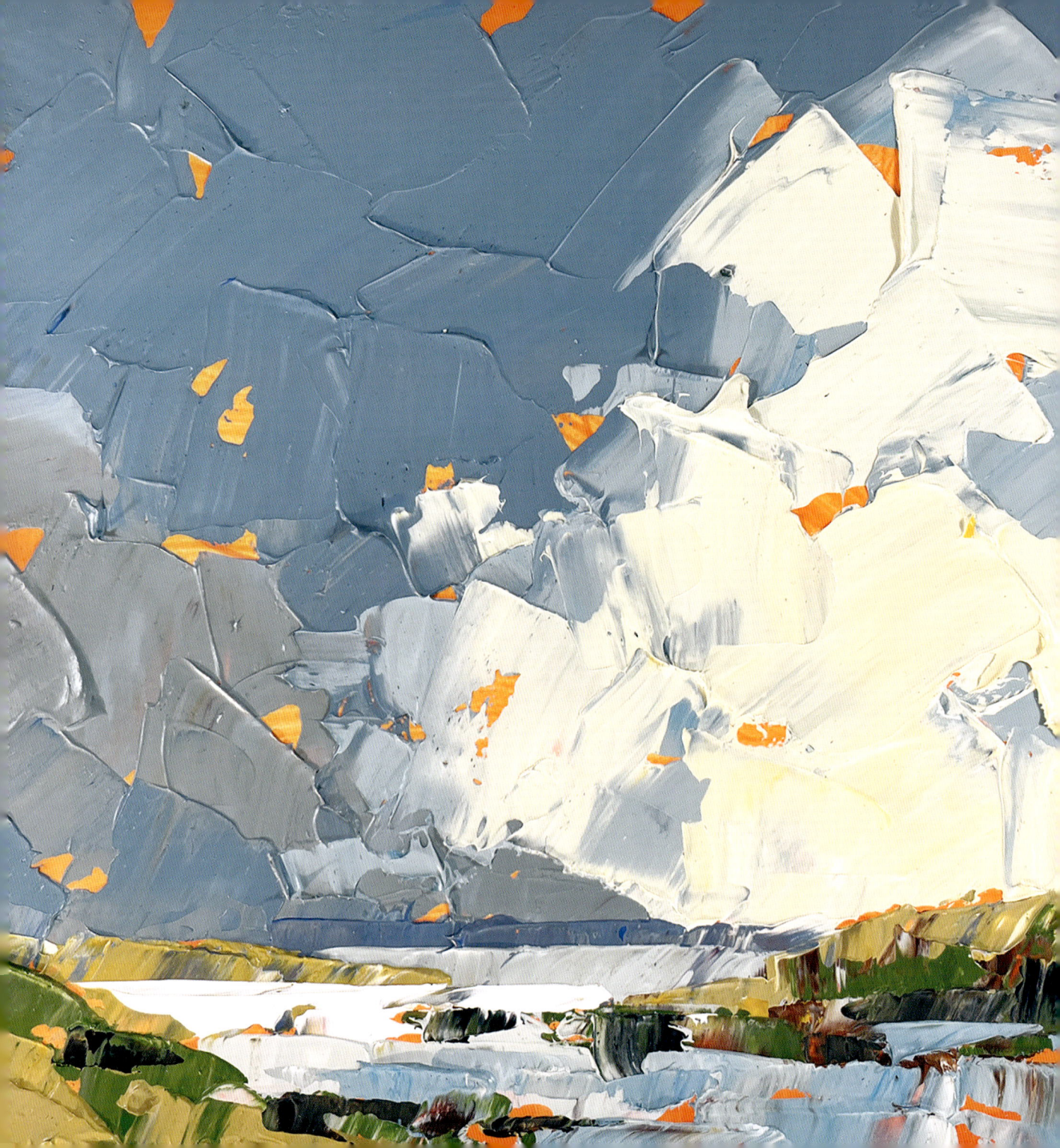

Lost & Found

Letters to the editor of the *Vineyard Gazette*
in 1847, 1921, 2002
(yesterday, tomorrow)
many with similar gripes:

The island has changed.
It's overrun, overdeveloped.
It isn't what it once was.

Human dramas come and go
dune sands ebb and flow
currents change, tides turn
and yet
and yet.

Today the island still stands
the plover nests
the wild rose blooms.

Today we still ask
what is worth holding on to?
And our answer is always the same:
this
this.

The Long Goodbye

Pulling up stakes and leaving the Island at summer's end
is the true mark of a year that's passed.
Birthdays and holidays are nice, but taking one last swim
in the late August Atlantic, knocking the sand out of the shoes
that have stood empty for weeks, and choosing a piece of sea glass
from the pile by the door to keep as a good luck charm
until we return—that's the end of another cherished summer
and the sign that the new year is about to begin.
Planes, trains and automobiles await,
but not until we cross over to the other side.

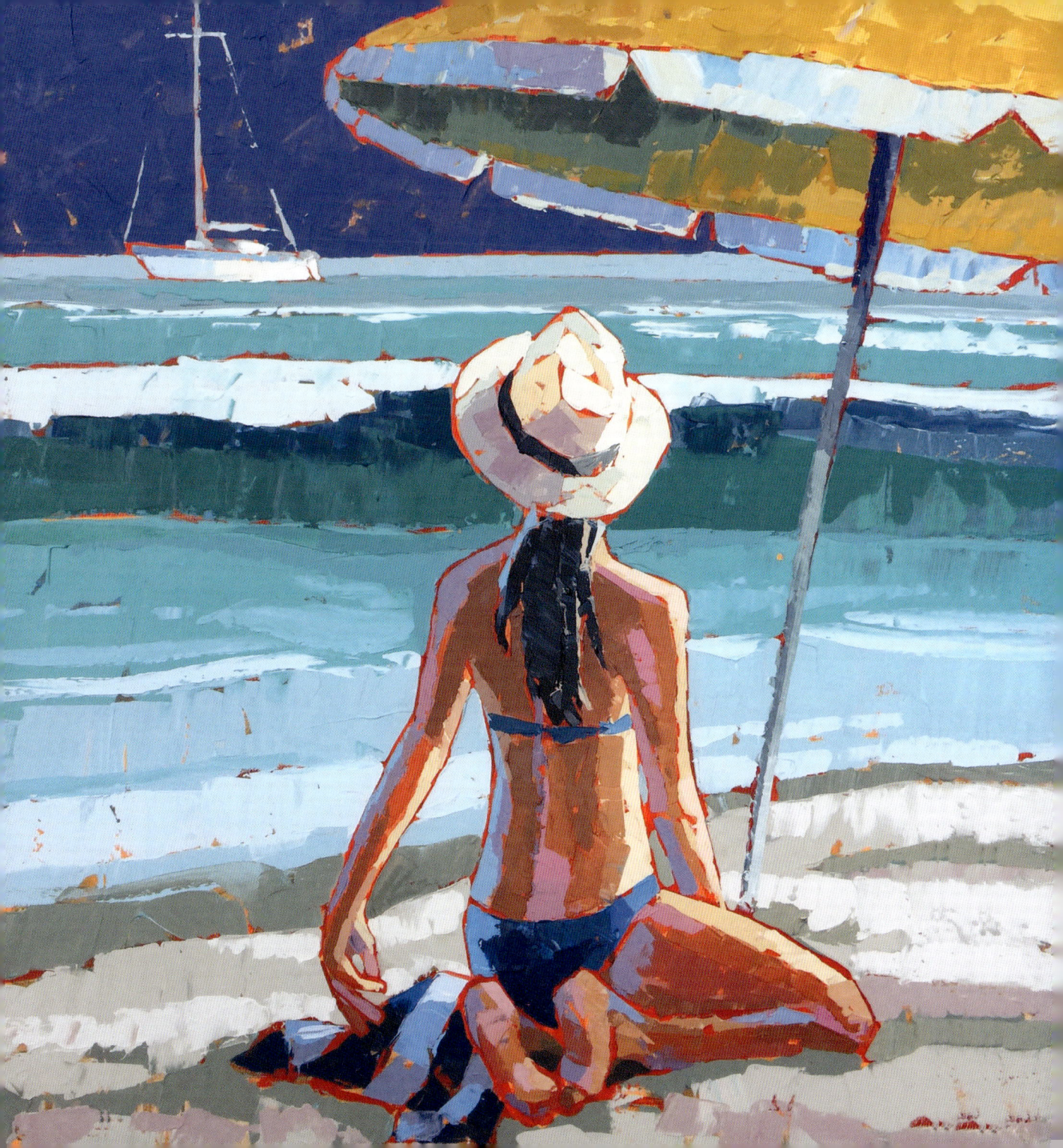

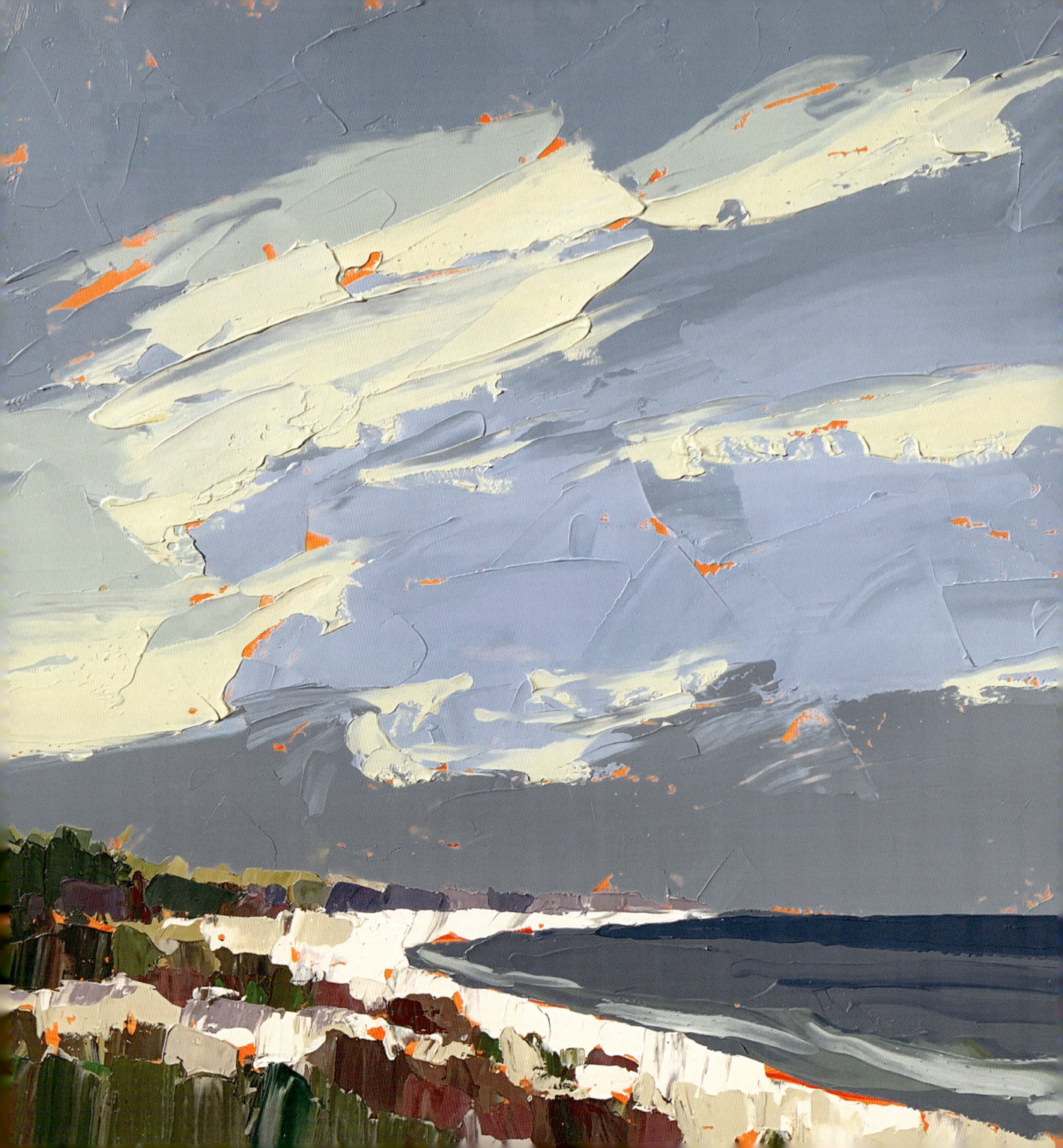

Off Season

The air is crisp
the snap of brush underfoot sharp
the lap of waves melodic
as we make our way
down the path.

Most years our cottage hibernates
only to wake when the weather warms.
But this year we manage to sneak away,
back to the Island, to our beach ritual
just with extra layers of fleece
and flasks of hot cider.

Winter is when this place
gets into our bones.
And the chill of it lingers,
a welcome memory to keep us cool
in the humid swelter
of next July's high-noon.

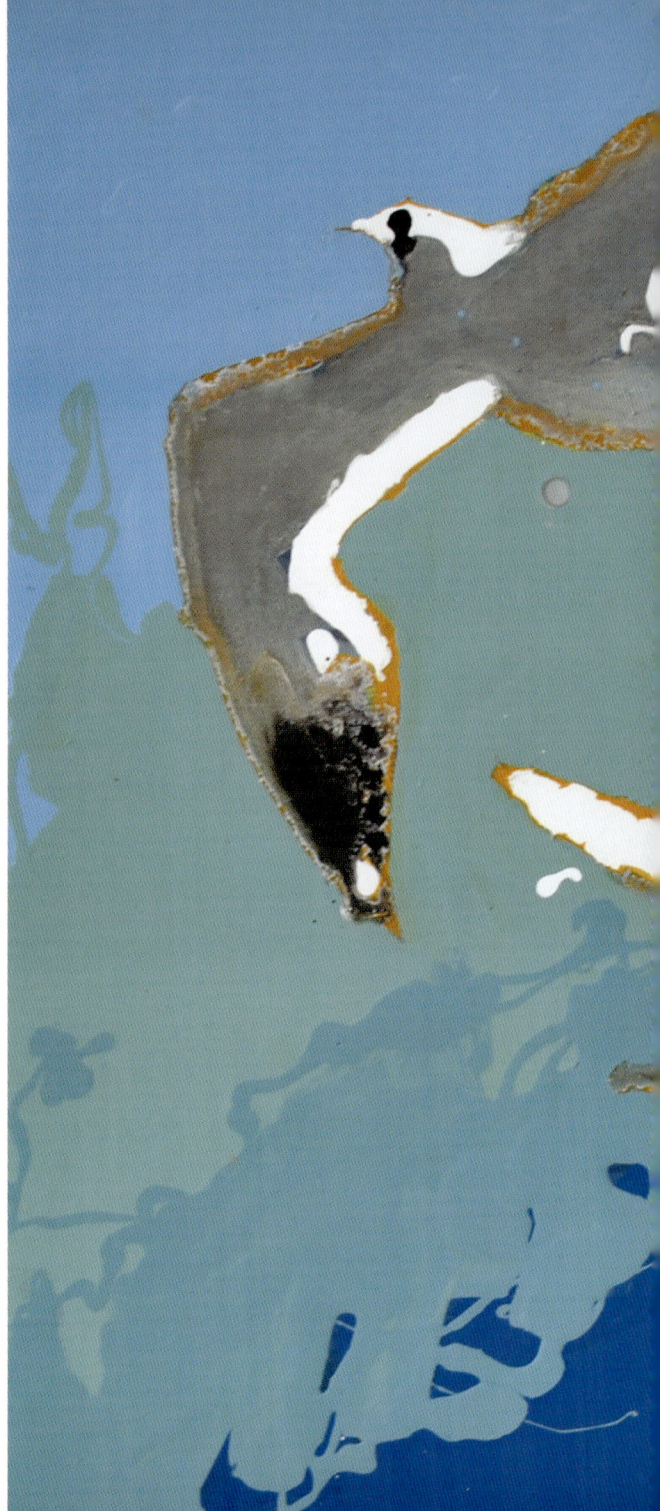

Soaring

in our dreams

we never need to learn

how to fly

we just know

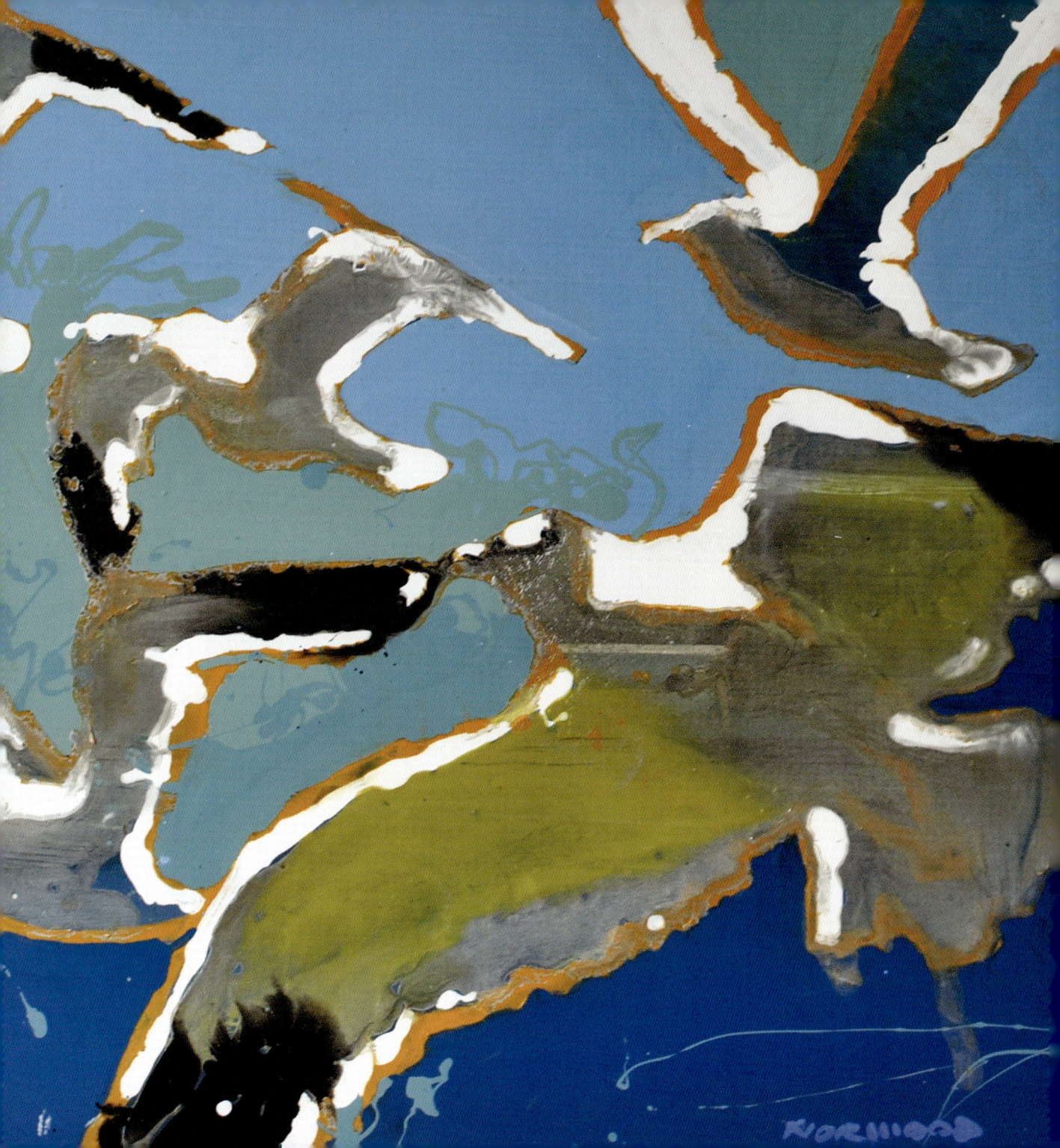

Artworks, Attributions, Inspirations

All paintings, unless noted, by Paul Norwood. All text, unless noted, by Liz and Paul Norwood.

Front Cover
Rounding the Chop, oil on board, 20 x 16 in

Inset Page, p.1
Sunset Shower, acrylic on canvas, 12 x 12 in

Title Page, pp.2–3
Lights on the Lake, acrylic on canvas, 60 x 60 in

Dedication Page, p.4
Red White in Blue, oil on canvas, 11 x 14 in

Come Away, p.7
Dueling Clouds, acrylic on board, 10 x 10 in

An Invitation, p.8
Over the Dunes, acrylic on board, 10 x 10 in

Are We There Yet?, p.11
Rounding the Chop, oil on board, 20 x 16 in

Simple Life, p.12
Menemsha Whites, oil on canvas, 10 x 8 in

Ode to Prepositions, p.14
Dune Study, acrylic on canvas, 12 x 12 in

Dropping In, p.17
Evening Guest, oil on board, 24 x 18 in

Double Page Painting, pp.18–19
Along the Pond, oil on board, 40 x 30 in

Jaws Bridge, p.21
Vineyard Summer, oil on canvas, 48 x 36 in

Great Pond, p.22
Painted Sky, acrylic on canvas, 20 x 20 in

General Store, p.24
Bookends, oil on board, 12 x 16 in

Ice House Pond, p.27
Chilmark Sunset, oil on board, 12 x 12 in

The Picnic, p.28
Painting by Laina Norwood: *Peasant's Feast*, acrylic on board, 14 x 20 in

Menemsha, p.31
Beached in Menemsha, oil on canvas, 20 x 14 in

Lambert's Cove, p.33
Evening Drama, acrylic on canvas, 48 x 48 in

The Inkwell, p.35
Inkwell Beach, acrylic on canvas, 12 x 12 in

Double Page Painting, pp.36–37
Menemsha Bay Dusk, oil on board, 36 x 48 in

First Island Corn, p.39
Spring Abstract, acrylic on canvas, 10 x 10 in

Honor System, p.41
Roadside Color, acrylic on board, 12 x 12 in

Water Color, p.43
Low Tide, acrylic on canvas, 11 x 11 in

Raw Bar, p.44
Island Tomatoes, oil on board, 16 x 16 in

Moonshadow, p.47
Moonshadow, acrylic on board, 10 x 10 in

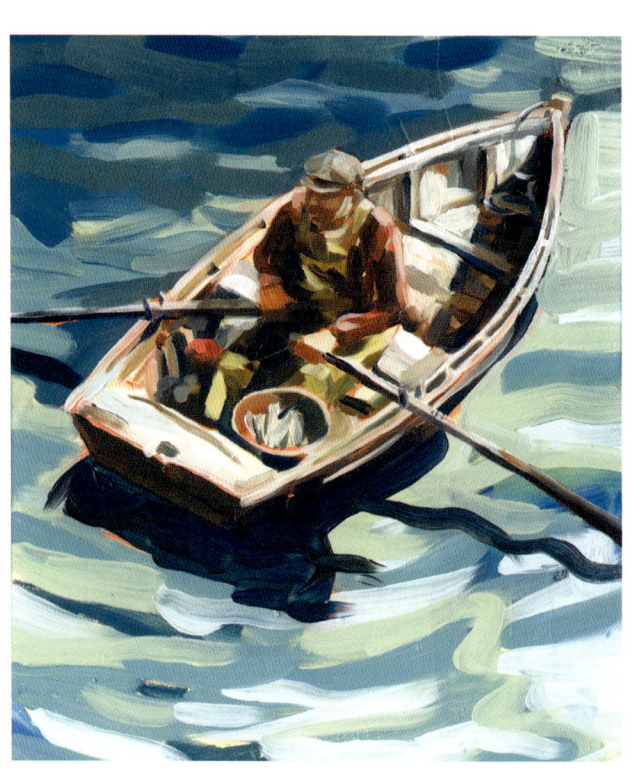

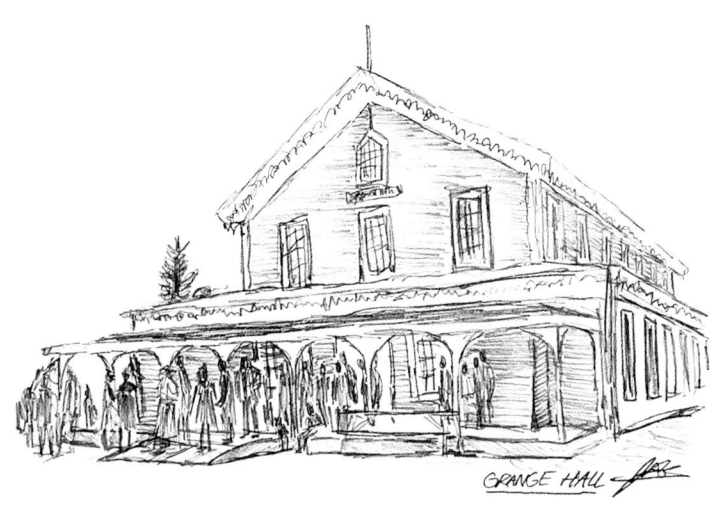

GRANGE HALL

Thank You

We'd like to thank all the people in our "village" who helped make this book a reality. Special shoutout to Linda Sparrowe and Katharine Harer for their thoughtful editing and guidance. To Brooke Warner and Laura Beers for placing signposts at critical intersections. To Elizabeth Eisenhauer and Paul Caval of the Eisenhauer Gallery for their friendship and support. To Stephanie Breitbard and the team at SBFA for so many years of West Coast success. To our friends Meghan McHugh, Bliss Broyard, Nico Israel, Ben Godley, John Longley, and Willow Older, for their insight and encouragement. To our kids, Jameson and Laina, for contributing content and sharing indelible Vineyard times with us. To our parents and the whole Thomas-Norwood family for inspiration, in person and spirit. And finally, to the island of Martha's Vineyard for welcoming us into the fold, for the honor of discovering her beauty, mystery and simple joys.

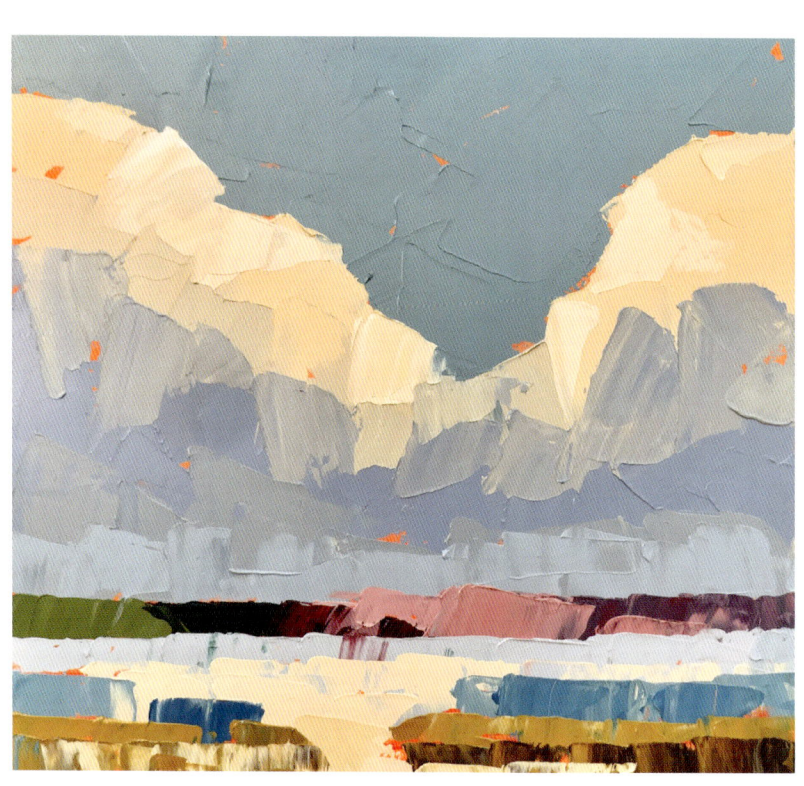

About the Authors

Paul Norwood, who grew up on the coast of Maine, decided early on that he'd rather paint the sea than fish from it. After a long career as an art director and creative director, he now devotes all his time to painting. In the past twenty-five years, Paul has developed a national client base and has exhibited his work in galleries and art fairs from Boston to San Francisco—and many places in between. On Martha's Vineyard, he's represented by the Eisenhauer Gallery in Edgartown.

Liz Norwood is a freelance editor and writer from the San Francisco Bay Area. She helps nonprofits, small businesses and creative types tell their stories and share their big ideas—from organic food companies and social justice organizations to community organizers, artists and authors.

With a home base in Mill Valley, California, Liz and Paul have been coming to Martha's Vineyard since the first summer they met. Their time here is a patchwork of painting and writing, working and playing, and exploring the island with their two kids, now grown and artists themselves.

Away to See: Martha's Vineyard is their first book together, with more books about other favorite places in the works.

www.awaytosee.com   instagram: away.to.see

Library of Congress Cataloging-in-Publication Data available.
ISBN: 978-1-68555-177-3
Ebook ISBN: 978-1-68555-635-8
LCCN: 2025911486

Manufactured in China.

10 9 8 7 6 5 4 3 2 1

The Collective Book Studio®
Oakland, California
www.thecollectivebook.studio